REINVENTING
THE
POST

REINVENTING THE POST

Changing Postal Thinking

Derek Osborn
Whatnext4u

LIBRI
PUBLISHING

First published in 2014 by Libri Publishing

Copyright © Derek Osborn

ISBN 978 1 909818 51 4

The right of Derek Osborn to be identified as the editor of this work has been asserted in accordance with the Copyright, Designs and Patents Act, 1988.

Authors retain copyright of individual chapters.

A CIP catalogue record for this book is available from The British Library

Design by Carnegie Publishing

Cover design by Helen Taylor

Printed in the UK by Short Run Press

Libri Publishing
Brunel House
Volunteer Way
Faringdon
Oxfordshire
SN7 7YR

Tel: +44 (0)845 873 3837

www.libripublishing.co.uk

CONTENTS

PREFACE

Dr Wolfgang Baier
GCEO, Singapore Post

The postal industry is pitched in a landscape of shifting goal posts. Steering clear of the potentially devastating impact of the tipping point in domestic mail volume decline is what drives our industry. This book on reinventing the post focuses on why the industry's approach to the market needs to change – and more urgently than ever. How we manage our postal businesses, the way we build and operate new businesses, even our very corporate DNA needs to be radically altered. The good news is that reinventing our postal industry will secure its future.

Transformation for postal players is not only inevitable, it needs to be accelerated. In the past, postal transformation was about rationalising the core business. However, postal players have now come to realise that there is life beyond letters – that a new 'core' can be built based on the growth of e-commerce and the related logistics services. It is hard to replicate a post's capability to reach every address on a daily basis at such a low cost.

At the same time, continuous market liberalisation has also brought new entrants into once exclusive markets. The playing field for postal players has become even more challenging. Postal players, big and small, need to be nimble to negotiate this rapidly changing postal terrain. We need to scan the horizon constantly for new revenue streams, particularly in the e-commerce and digital arena. We can work towards delivering a new post.

As we construct the new core and reinvent the post, there are many questions that emerge: How can we redesign our operating model to handle more volumetric parcels? Are letterboxes still the only way to receive letters? How do inventive technologies such as 3D printing and drones play a part in the new scheme of things? And there are many more. Integral to all of these issues, however, are three main areas of focus: digital customers, e-commerce and our people.

ENABLING THE DIGITAL CONSUMERS

Our customers are our lifeline. We need resources and analytics to understand their lifestyle changes. Alongside these, we also need to innovate to meet new customer needs and manage their increasingly high expectations. Ironically, while we may have fewer letters to deliver, we may also have more addresses to reach. SingPost, like many of its counterparts, is committed to its national service obligations. We deliver to every corner of Singapore's main and outlying islands. The quality of our customer service has to meet high regulatory standards. We have been investing to adhere to these Quality of Service markers, which are in fact among the most stringent in the world. Customer-centricity and building relationships have become our corporate mantra. At SingPost, an integral part of our transformation has been to entrench customer-centricity as deeply and widely into our corporate psyche and structures as possible. We do this by listening to our customers via social media and anticipating their requirements through agile, data-driven systems. We need to ensure a seamless customer experience by fine-tuning technology and processes. Customer-driven innovation needs to be at the heart of the every postal transformation.

The extensive influence of social media has become a driving force. To understand digital customer preferences, we need to understand how they use social media. Social media progressively connects consumers of all demographic groups and increasingly shapes customer preferences. In Asia especially, we are seeing buying decisions influenced by blog posts, online forums and message boards. As postal companies we need to enable the digital customer. Conditions now allow for this – given the high mobile and Internet adoption rates, ASEAN has already an estimated 160-million online citizens. For now, this is 30m and 40m fewer than the EU and US respectively, but it is set to grow. This is the age of mobile commerce – influenced by social media. Posts need to gear their engagement with their customers via digital touchpoints. Online, web kiosks and mobile channels empower today's customers to access services 24/7. There is not a minute in the day now in which our customers can be left unattended.

EMBRACING E-COMMERCE

Globally, e-commerce has been growing exponentially – and Asia Pacific has caught on. Last year, the US dominated the e-commerce market in terms of sales, though the scene is set to change. Asia-Pacific will claim more than 44% of digital buyers worldwide in 2014. This year alone, B2C e-commerce sales are expected to reach $525 billion in the region, compared with $482 billion in North America. By 2017, Asia Pacific e-commerce sales are expected to cross US$1 trillion.

This is a once-in-a-lifetime opportunity for postal companies across the globe. With our multiple touchpoints and local delivery networks, we have an advantage. We need to use it now or it may be lost forever. Integrating postal services with e-commerce solutions is the key.

The emergence of more and more omni-channel commerce solutions, bridging physical retail, web, social and mobile channels, poses both opportunities and threats for posts. On the one hand, it drives e-commerce volumes; on the other, in-store pickup could cut posts out of the e-commerce value chain. To stay relevant, we have to find a way to plug ourselves into the emerging omni-channel ecosystem via integrated e-commerce logistics solutions. With these basics in place, posts can then also leverage opportunities such as O2O (online to offline and offline to online) where posts can be 'the arms and legs' on the ground for businesses.

COMMITTING TO OUR PEOPLE

At its core, ours is a people business. You can invest in the most intelligent technologies, but if your last-mile delivery is not reliable, you are soon out of business. We depend on our people to deliver a good service. The importance of people can never be over-emphasised. We need to have people with the right mindset. For this, postal leaders need to put in place a clear vision, with relevant values, to drive the right culture.

Each postal operator will have its own vision and leverage on their core strengths and opportunities. In my first year in SingPost, we restructured the business into five business pillars under a transformation programme. Our objective was clear: to be *'the regional leader in e-commerce logistics and trusted communications'*. The first task was to rally the SingPost team, from senior management to our frontline postmen and delivery staff on the ground, in order to venture into uncharted e-commerce and digital waters. We needed the entire organisation to row together.

As leaders in the postal industry, we need to engage people and communicate the necessity and the value of our transformation programmes. It is important to engage with all levels of our people in the organisation. I also advocate taking an inclusive approach, and creating avenues to help lower-income staff and their families cope with changes, including the rising cost of living. If this isn't done, they will be in danger of getting left behind.

CONCLUSION

Many postal operators have already been making good progress towards reinventing themselves. They have identified new growth frontiers and are going for it. For SingPost, we see e-commerce logistics as our next growth trajectory. We have been investing to serve the digital generation by building an integrated end-to-end e-commerce logistics network in Asia.

But the true power of posts is our ability to cooperate and create competitive integrated cross-border networks. Only if we are united and work together can we make the postal industry an integral part of the future digital economy.

As we reinvent our respective postal organisations and the industry, we rightly feel a growing sense of achievement as we see more and more 'ticks' on our transformation checklist. Yet there can be no rest for us in the postal industry. We are on an on-going and sometimes exhilarating journey. During the course of our vital reinvention, I am often asked by SingPosters 'We have worked hard, achieved much, when will our transformation be over, when can we stop?' My answer is that postal transformation never ends. We need to keep reinventing ourselves every single day to stay relevant and remain an enduring company in a very exciting industry.

ACKNOWLEDGEMENTS

This new volume builds on the momentum and success of the three books in the series *The Future is in the Post* and of the first edition of *Reinventing the Post* which has been distributed and read throughout the postal world. Once again, I would like to acknowledge the support, suggestions and encouragement which I have received from people in many different parts of the wider postal industry who have read the previous books and urged me to continue.

In particular, I would like to thank all those who have willingly and enthusiastically contributed to this volume and who have been ready to share ideas and insights from their experience.

As with the other volumes, I want to express my gratitude to UKIP Media & Events Ltd, organisers of PostExpo, and in particular to Matt Gunn for his continued support and belief in this idea of an annual book to showcase the industry and stimulate robust discussion about the key challenges it faces. I would also like to thank Paul Jervis and John Sivak of Libri Publishing for maintaining their unswerving confidence in this continuing project.

For this latest volume, I have also been assisted in the task of editing by Jacob Johnsen and Graeme Lee, for which I am very grateful.

This volume is dedicated to support and encourage all those who work in the postal sector, for whom the landscape is changing and for whom the opportunities not only remain but increase and expand, as the postal sector reinvents itself for new markets and generations.

Finally, I would like to thank my family for their continued support, despite my busy schedule.

Derek Osborn

May 2014

THE EDITOR

Derek Osborn is an enthusiastic, innovative and inspiring business coach, management trainer and workshop facilitator. Through his company, Whatnext4u, he works globally – focusing mainly on business strategy, human resource development, innovation, leadership and change management. He has wide experience and expert knowledge of the postal business, with 22 years in senior management previously in Royal Mail and over 17 years working internationally across the postal industry. He is passionate about creating opportunities and engaging platforms for collaboration to share knowledge, ideas and benchmark best practice so as to promote the industry, develop capability, encourage learning and foster innovation. Derek has coached many people and organisations, including governments, national postal operators and other postal stakeholders, working with them to improve operations and efficiency, develop greater customer focus and innovative strategies, as well as to lead change and transformation. He specialises in devising and delivering bespoke senior-executive programmes, forums and workshops. With Dr K. Sund, Derek co-edited three volumes of *The Future is in the Post*. This is the second edition of *Reinventing the Post* – the first was published in October 2013 and launched in Vienna at Post Expo. He can be contacted via: derekosborn@whatnext4u.com.

INTRODUCTION TO THIS BOOK

Derek Osborn
Whatnext4u

'Change' is a word that recurs throughout this book – indeed it is in the sub-title, *Changing Postal Thinking*. We all now live in a state of *permanent change*, both in our private and public lives. So we need constantly to re-assess and re-orientate ourselves in many different ways, to be able to adapt and thrive in the complex world of the twenty-first century. The postal industry is in the same situation (as is every other sector), with virtually everything changing around it and also within it.

In previous books, I have used the term 'postal landscape'; but a landscape tends to change much more slowly over time, due to its comparative solidity. Perhaps a better metaphor to use now to describe the ever-changing environment is the *postal seascape*. Out in the big oceans, the seascape changes constantly, influenced by the wind and weather, tides and currents. It is often difficult to get your bearings because, unlike on land, there may be no directional reference points.

Most people in the postal industry would readily accept that, compared with the last few hundred years, we are now in *uncharted waters* and, in most cases, without a clear destination for which to aim. Depending on your outlook, being afloat in unchartered waters without knowing where you are going can either be worrying or exciting – probably a bit of both. If this picture resonates with you then you will enjoy reading the short chapter by Maurizio Puppo in which he describes the challenge of leading the posts today, when the destination is unknown.

To continue with this metaphor, it could be said that this book (and the previous edition) are in some ways charting the *tides and currents* that are shaping the current seascape, in the knowledge that any of these may be overtaken within a short time by a new swell or even the sighting of a land mass that could provide some temporary refuge or a more durable foundation for future business.

Another thought about the sea would be to equate the *turbulent surface* of the water with the vast number of digital applications and new technology ideas that seem to bob up all the time. João Melo describes this bewildering context well in his chapter on new lifestyles. Most of us can easily recognise the relentless tidal wave of new gadgets, applications and Internet- or technology-driven ideas that we are confronted with every day. This ebb and flow can be deeply disturbing and disruptive for conventional businesses with cycles of business planning that usually take much longer than a week and business operating models that cannot be adjusted in an afternoon.

This would all be very disconcerting were it not for one way of looking at the strength and competence of the traditional postal sector. It can be viewed as a *strong anchor*, rooted in the physical assets and capabilities that have made it so powerful in the past. Comprehensive address information, granular locational knowledge, trusted-intermediary status, the ability to authenticate and verify, door-to-door delivery ability, security, coverage and reach, logistics expertise, presence in all the communities and with all customers, small and large – these are just some of the features that enable the post to be the perfect anchor for more risky and transient digital solutions on the market – most of which will come and go but are not as durable as the physical post.

In the rush to be 'on the digital market', posts should not neglect their key strengths and the opportunity for which they are uniquely positioned, which is to be the solid and stabilising anchor, not just for themselves but for others. Indeed, the vulnerabilities of e-mail, data security, power sources, Internet connections, technology failures and incompatible systems make it extremely prudent to have a tried and tested durable back up for business continuity – a strong anchor for difficult times.

In describing how postal thinking is changing, this book aims to provide small glimpses into what is happening across the 'postal seascape'. These short insights and vignettes are probably insufficient to chart a complete *map*, but helpful to locate some points to *navigate* between.

The first of the seven sections describes how the market is changing and identifies some of the currents that are swirling around. The second section then explores what kind of leadership is needed in this context – where collaboration is essential and no business stands by itself.

Needless to say, posts do not just need to think differently but also to change the way that they operate: this is elaborated in the third section. If operational changes are only about changing processes or procedures, they may make some difference; but to ride the waves more successfully, the whole culture of the posts needs to change and that is not achieved easily or quickly – as can be seen in the fourth section.

Section five includes examples of how governance in the whole sector is also changing, through regulatory and legislative intervention but also due to market forces and privatisation, and examines the question of where this leaves universal service. In the sixth section, the impact of technology and the digital revolution inform some different perspectives on the challenges and dilemmas faced by the industry.

Finally, contributions in the last section turn to the future and how that might look for the postal sector or for players within it.

How can this stormy sea be navigated? What seems to be a good strategy? My personal conclusion is that we need to be *continually reinventing the post* and I encourage you to enjoy reading the chapters in this book, considering and discussing the questions. Then you can play your part in this epic journey – I hope we make some exciting discoveries along the way!

SECTION 1
CHANGING POSTAL MARKET

Derek Osborn

The changing market in which the posts operate is a key *driver* and is changing postal thinking in a big way. There are many factors that are influencing these changes, some of which are intentional changes designed to liberalise markets and introduce different regulatory regimes; but others are more pervasive changes to the lifestyles, communication patterns and social behaviour of consumers – all of which are underpinned by the inexorable advance of the digital revolution and fuelled by new applications of technology which seem to be appearing at an ever-faster rate.

This section is about how the postal industry is reacting or adapting to these significant market changes, and the extent to which, given the ubiquitous nature of postal-service provision and wide brand recognition in most countries, postal businesses can also influence and shape the market.

Dr Herbert-Michael Zapf explores the global context in which the industry operates, highlighting some of the successful strategies that have been adopted – including process optimisation, diversification and the maximising of potential still to be gained from existing business. However, he also addresses the challenges and opportunities arising from the digital economy, recognising that there are big implications for posts if they are to build on their traditional customer proximity in order to develop more innovative services and define new roles for themselves.

Jeff Sibio emphasises that, in a changing market, the imperative is to understand the customers, the needs they have and the experiences they want. One way to do this is to behave like a new entrant, if only to 'shake off' old thinking and welcome disruptive innovation. He discusses how posts can explore the provision of layers of value-added services, particularly across the e-commerce value chain. Finally, he encourages posts to discover what they are best at and to use that to differentiate themselves in the market.

Laraine Balk Hope and **Jean Philippe Ducasse** consider the outlook for advertising mail in the new market conditions. They explain that the strategic importance of direct mail for posts is increasing, and that it will continue to play a key role in multi-channel communication, complimenting other forms of digital engagement and personalised interaction with customers in highly targeted and customised ways. With intelligent use of big data, this leads ultimately to customising the 'Internet of postal things' – all to help customers, but also to respect their privacy.

Finally, **Erwin Lenhardt** maintains that, driven by the growth of e-commerce, the traditional postal market is migrating into a logistics market. Logistics clearly provides many opportunities for B2B and B2C sectors, and he argues that for both the key to success lies in good logistics IT systems and solutions which can operate on different platforms.

Overall results of the postal industry show, however, that strategies of the postal industry to adapt to changing realities through active innovation and process optimisation have paid off. There is a vibrant growth agenda for the postal sector.

CHANGING POSTAL MARKETS

Dr Herbert-Michael Zapf

President and CEO, International Post Corporation

INTRODUCTION

Although posts throughout the world are faced with widely diverging economic conditions and business models, most are confronted with the same challenges of declining mail volumes and the need to enter into new business areas. Overall results of the postal industry show, however, that strategies of the postal industry to adapt to changing realities through active innovation and process optimisation have paid off. There is a vibrant growth agenda for the postal sector. This is confirmed by the good performance of the postal operators listed in the stock markets.

Fully reaping the growth potential implies that posts both maximise the value of existing services – by optimising processes and increasing efficiency – and invest in new business areas. To realise that, posts should have sufficient flexibility to adapt their processes and develop new business models.

PROCESS OPTIMISATION AND DIVERSIFICATION LEADS TO OVERALL REVENUE GROWTH

Overall postal industry revenue reached €422.6bn in 2012, showing an overall revenue increase of 3.9% despite continued mail-volume decline.[1] Mail revenue fell by €1.59bn, while combined revenue from parcels and express, financial services,

---

and logistics and freight increased by €8.4bn. With a 6.4% revenue increase, parcels and express represented the main growth driver for posts in 2012. The degree of revenue diversification has continued to increase for the industry as a whole as posts have been actively pursuing growth opportunities in other key business areas, notably parcels and express, postal financial services, and logistics and freight. Diversification increased significantly between 2010 and 2012, with the revenue share of mail falling to 47.1%. The combined revenue share of parcels and express, logistics and freight, and postal financial services now amounts to 45.1%, representing an increase of 4.7% since 2010.

Different trends can be observed from one world region to another. Revenue growth was strongest in emerging economies such as the BRICS countries and Asia Pacific while average revenue declined in Europe and North America. Corporate performance has been strongly influenced by economic conditions across the respective regions and the rate of Internet penetration, but also by the degree of diversification of postal operators. While Europe's share of overall postal revenue remained stable, the North American share declined and BRICS's share increased. Postal revenue growth has been the strongest in those markets where growth in e-commerce sales has been the highest and reliance on traditional mail revenue is the lowest.

While mail revenue declined at the industry level, many posts still experienced growth in this segment in 2012, particularly those operating in BRICS and Asia Pacific. Unaddressed admail volumes remain stable and continue to grow in certain markets, in contrast to priority and non-priority letters and addressed admail.

These figures allow us to identify some clear trends in the key growth opportunities for the years to come.

MAXIMISING POTENTIAL OF EXISTING BUSINESS THROUGH DIRECT MAIL

The postal industry is experiencing challenging times, but there is an opportunity to reposition mail by connecting with today's global consumer needs and demonstrating the benefits of direct mail in online marketing campaigns.

Recent marketing research in the United States shows that US$600bn of sales revenue was generated in the US by US$50bn of spending on direct mail[2] in 2012. This shows that direct mail has the best return on investment of all media and that it therefore has a key potential in direct marketing campaigns. Direct mail is often integrated as part of a multi-channel campaign and has proven to be effective in combination with other direct marketing channels, including online tools.

Over the past years, many posts have developed a direct marketing portfolio embracing both addressed and unaddressed mail. For example, PostNL has been developing cross-media campaigns featuring addressed and unaddressed advertising campaigns in combination with new advertising services for mobile devices. Deutsche Post DHL is offering advertisers a cross-media solution that marries direct mail with personalised online messages through the use of QR and alpha-numeric codes. The post also carries out automated response management and geotagging in real time, providing customers with information about the status and success of their campaign.

CHALLENGES AND OPPORTUNITIES FROM THE DIGITAL ECONOMY

The increased digitisation of the economy is one of the main reasons for the decline in traditional mail services. However, digitisation is also the driving force behind e-commerce growth, which offers posts great growth opportunities.

The development of e-commerce is undoubtedly recognised as one of the major trends of the economy in the recent years, bringing significant changes to the retail sector. In times of slow economic growth, e-commerce is increasingly seen as a major engine of growth and jobs.

Total B2C e-commerce sales have amounted to slightly over €1tn in 2013. With sales amounting to €350bn in 2013, Europe was the largest e-commerce market and showed an average year-on-year growth of 19% compared to 2012. Eastern Europe and in particular Russia have registered growth rates well above the average (up to 35%). E-commerce sales in 2013 amounted to €318bn in North America, seeing a yearly growth rate of 18%.

Nevertheless, the real e-commerce revolution is Asian. Asia Pacific was the second-largest e-commerce market with sales of €338bn in 2013, but with a year-on-year growth rate of 30%, Asia Pacific is set to overtake Europe as the largest e-commerce market in the coming years, and will probably soon account for 40% of the global e-commerce market. Smartphones, mobile e-commerce and, increasingly, social commerce through Facebook and Twitter are driving this unprecedented growth. In China, the e-retail giant Tmall, which handles 7m packages a day, is reporting growth of 100% year on year – and this has been the case for the past three years.

The trend in China today is for the digital-native generation to purchase everything online, including household products. Consumer behaviour in emerging markets like China offers insights into potential trends in other regions, such as Europe and North America. With the emergence of a new middle class with an increasing purchase power, evolving buying habits, the ongoing penetration of Internet and easier online payment systems, the Asian share of the global e-commerce market will only grow further. How this will affect the global e-commerce landscape and how leading global posts should get involved are key questions.

With an expected growth of more than 10% a year, cross-border e-commerce still represents an untapped potential for the postal sector. The e-commerce market is highly dynamic and characterised by the rapid emergence of new business models and players moving up and down the value chain. Posts are best placed to exploit the potential of e-commerce, but they must continue to innovate in order to match changing consumers' and e-sellers' needs and be able to compete successfully in the market. Barriers are still preventing small- and medium-sized companies from selling across borders. Addressing those could boost cross-border e-commerce by up to 75% by 2020.

Competition in the e-commerce delivery market is fierce and rapidly evolving, driving posts to innovate continuously and develop new offerings. Large international e-retailers are investing in their own delivery models, such as pick-up points and lockers, as well as local warehouses, which reduce the need for cross-border delivery. Freight-forwarders and consolidators partner with large retailers to offer international shipping by consolidating domestic deliveries. They offer fulfilment, shipping, duties and customs clearance. They act as an intermediary between the e-retailer and the delivery provider and transform the delivery into a commodity while putting pressure on prices.

With the evolution of the market, consumers are increasingly looking for convenience and speed. In this context, a shift is observed from delivery to collection, with the development of alternatives to home delivery such as collection points, networks or parcel lockers. This is a trend that postal operators have also embraced actively over the past years, namely by investing in their own parcel-locker networks. Several posts have launched their own such networks, including Deutsche Post DHL, Le Groupe La Poste, bpost and Swiss Post.

Amazon, Google and eBay all offer same-day delivery services, which respond to a growing consumer demand for convenience and speed. One such same-day delivery service is eBay Now, which is currently on trial in the San Francisco Bay Area and offers a one-hour delivery service for goods purchased through the app for a US$5 delivery charge. Same-day delivery remains a niche market at the moment, with limited-scope pilot projects and premium services limited to certain goods, such as fresh products. However, the impact of same-day delivery on consumer expectations and on delivery times should not be underestimated.

Several posts, such as bpost and Japan Post, are exploiting this opportunity and have developed a portal through which consumers can purchase their weekly groceries online and have them delivered together with services such as dry cleaning in one consolidated delivery made by the post.

In order fully to reap the potential of e-commerce and to respond best to the needs of e-retailers – and in particular SMEs – posts are aiming to be active across the e-commerce value chain from procurement, website development and marketing, to transport, customs clearance, payment fulfilment, delivery, returns and customer service. Several postal operators have launched strategies in this direction.

When it comes to cross-border e-commerce, surveys show that a lack of consistent visibility and delivery options, and complex returns procedures, prevent consumers and e-sellers from shopping and selling online. By responding to the needs of consumers for cross-border track and trace and a reliable cross-border e-commerce delivery service, posts can become more competitive in the cross-border market.

Achieving this objective will only be possible through stronger integration and interoperability of postal networks. IPC, as a leading technical-service provider for posts worldwide, is playing a supporting role by building the technical and operational solutions which will enable the interconnection of postal networks and further boost cross-border e-commerce.

CONCLUSION

The postal industry has been through radical changes over recent years, demonstrating its capacity to adapt to new realities by defending its existing business and entering new areas. The postal industry is now reaching a new unique milestone. The average contribution of mail to postal-group revenue is now below 50% and many posts are reaching the tipping point at which other business segments, such as e-commerce delivery, will overtake mail in terms of revenue. Such a transformation will not only have implications for the organisation, the business models and the workforce of posts, but also for their identities. The proximity to people, especially in rural and remote areas, through mail delivery has forged the postal identity and has always been one of the posts' key assets in increasingly competitive markets. Posts can build on this customer proximity to develop new innovative services and define new roles for themselves, such as providing assistance services to citizens. The key challenge for posts in the coming years will therefore be to maintain their strong identity and visibility among citizens while continuing their successful diversification.

QUESTION FOR THOUGHT AND DISCUSSION

To what extent is the evolving market shaping the strategic development of the postal industry and how can the posts shape how the market evolves?

Listening to your customers, determining who they are and what experience they desire, can provide significant insight on how you can determine what your best is. You can then use this to behave like a new entrant in the market.

BEHAVING LIKE A NEW ENTRANT IN THE MARKET

Jeff Sibio

Intermec by Honeywell

INTRODUCTION

Postal services have long provided the delivery of letters and parcels, but these services are under significant pressure in today's transforming business environment. The challenge to these well-established, and in many cases dominant, postal service providers, in their given geographies, is that they are finding themselves with a new imperative to evolve quickly to address the competitive market forces and opportunities. Dealing with this challenging new landscape is not optional. Traditional posts with mature and value-rich operations must attack the new business challenge head-on by approaching their business in a new and innovative manner, much like a 'new entrant' would do.

Utilising customer-centric approaches to business will be the key to success. Companies that tackle business in the manner of new entrants will be a mix of true new entrants, such as start-ups and migrants from adjacent sectors, and existing players that break out of the old dusty mould and achieve 'differentiated innovation'.

How do posts around the world move from providing an established service to behaving like a new entrant in the market?

Two factors are crucial to developing and implementing this new perspective: embracing evolutions in the supply chain such as e-commerce and focusing on customer experience. We must ask ourselves: who is our customer and what is the experience they desire, and why? How do we evolve from the business of yesterday to what our customers want today? How do we give customers what they want, when they want it? And how do we separate out what they want from what they need and are willing, ultimately, to pay a premium for? One has to build on the other.

CUSTOMISING THE CUSTOMER EXPERIENCE

Today's customer expectations are higher than ever and it is imperative that we understand these as well as know who our customer is. Identifying the experience our customers want will unlock the answer to how we can deliver value and provide unique, innovative ways to reach our customer.

How do we do this? We must get to know our customers first and find out what they truly want without relying on traditional assumptions. Then we can work out how we need to evolve to give our customers what they want today.

WHO IS OUR CUSTOMER AND WHAT IS THE EXPERIENCE THEY DESIRE?

Identifying the 'ideal' customer experience is complicated; however, it's an absolute necessity. Customers' needs and expectations can change daily. When it comes to identifying what they desire, these factors come into play: 'one size' fits none; choice is a mandate; convenience is critical; and what works for me does not work for you. We must identify and meet these varying, demanding needs in effective, efficient and profitable ways.

If we leave the new market to the new entrants, we are destined to die with the old market. It's time to move on. How do we do this? Focus on a solution value, not a technology or business model. This is hard because it means embracing change and being a provocateur of change; but it avoids becoming a victim of evolution.

Let's look at the example of Kodak. George Eastman began innovating in the field of photography in 1878 when he was one of the first people to demonstrate the convenience of gelatin dry plates over the wet-plate photography prevalent at that time. He continued experimenting and introducing new products, including the first transparent photographic 'film' as we know it today. In 1888, the name Kodak was born with the introduction of its first camera on the market, thus introducing snapshot photography as millions of photographers know it today[1]. Many of us remember posing in front of a 'Kodak Moment' sign for an embarrassing family photo when we were young.

Nearly 100 years later, Kodak sold 90% of all photographic film and 85% of all cameras in the United States[2]. Everyone seemed to know the term 'Kodak Moment.' Yet today, Kodak is all but gone from the consumer marketplace even though it invented the first digital camera in 1975[3]. What went wrong?

Kodak was 'married' to its photographic technology (film and chemicals) instead of giving its customers and potential new consumers the experience and value they wanted. Had Kodak focused on delivering the true high-quality experience customers wanted instead of being wed to a technological approach, it could still be a significant player influencing the digital market today.

In the 2013 edition of *Reinventing the Post*, we studied the example of Apple's disruptive innovation. It was not the invention of the iPod that created success for Apple: it was the introduction of iTunes, which transformed the process for delivering digital content. Apple did not invent any of the core technologies at that time; instead, it created a more valuable offering by integrating its knowledge of customer desires for an easier customer experience in finding, purchasing and loading music onto a portable music player[4].

Some posts are taking this disruptive innovation approach by examining what they currently have in their possession, such as delivery expertise and unused space, and transforming themselves by using these resources to deliver the best experience for their customers today. For example, some posts are turning empty warehouse space once used for high volumes of letters into fulfilment service centres for fast-moving e-commerce items. This meets customer demand for getting what they want, when they want it; and because e-retailers can keep these products closer to customers, they can offer extremely quick delivery, perhaps even on the very afternoon the customer places the order.

1   Kodak Company History, available from: www.kodak.com/ek/US/en/Our_Company/ History_of_Kodak/Milestones_-_chronology/1878-1929.htm

2   *Telegraph*, 'The End of Our Kodak Moment', 19 January 2012, available from: www.telegraph. co.uk/women/mother-tongue/9025257/The-end-of-our-Kodak-moment.html

3   Forbes, 'Kodak Failed By Asking The Wrong Questions', 23 January 2012, available from: www. forbes.com/sites/avidan/2012/01/23/kodak-failed-by-asking-the-wrong-marketing-question/

4   Lowendmac.com, 'A History of the iPod 2000 to 2004', accessed February 2013

There are a few key principles that are understood by organisations that seem to achieve this level of customer intimacy best. First, the more intimate you get with a customer type, the more specific and valuable you are able to make your offerings – and moreover, that value and differentiation can directly relate to profits. This is especially true if you are able to position yourself as the gateway to that customer type, thus driving a unique value for your services by allowing your shipper customers to access their needed end user via your services. Second, since one size does not fit all, there may be niche customer wants that cannot be accomplished. Understanding these limitations and maintaining focus on profitable offerings are key to long-term success. A great example of this focus is the target-market segmentation which several posts have utilised to become expert in specific supply-chain functions, thus carving out defendable positions with a depth of knowledge that makes their offering unique.

E-COMMERCE IS NOW

Once, not so long ago, e-commerce was considered the future. This has changed: e-commerce is today. Businesses are leveraging e-commerce as a significant answer to the customer demand of 'how do I get what I want, when I want it? – and I want it now!'

And customers have high expectations when it comes to delivery: they want choice, instant access to tracking, proactive communication and easy returns. This may seem like a tall order, but some businesses are meeting these expectations – and exceeding them by offering additional delivery choices, such as time-specific slots and locations, and same-day services. An example of an e-commerce organisation that has found its niche and is exploiting it well is Zappos.com. Originally known for the speed with which it delivered shoes, Zappos has evolved to meet the shopping needs of its customers. With its easy and, perhaps most importantly, free returns, customers will order four or five pairs of shoes to find the perfect fit, keep that one and return the others. Arguably, Zappos.com is now known more for its 'beloved return policy' and process than its shoes.

This is only one case of a company which has carved out and claimed a defendable niche. Based on this example, a question for posts might be: how are we enabling retailers, manufacturers, distributors and e-commerce organisations to expand and thrive in this Internet economy? Is it our niche to be the go-to e-commerce connection for our market? Are we providing unique offerings that enable our customers to deliver the customer experience they want for their end-user customers? Are we providing our customers with the conduit they need to reach their customers in a way that excites their end-users, thus helping our customers grow their business?

Many organisations are realising that adjusting to meet customer demands means giving our customers access to the markets they need in order to thrive, or providing access to the suppliers that customers need in order to grow. For your customers, it may be that emerging markets will drive their growth. Many posts around the world are realising this need to provide their domestic customers access to emerging markets and the growth opportunities they hold. To accomplish this, we need to make serving emerging markets easy for our domestic customers, to expand their markets – and grow our businesses. And emerging markets may mean access to a new geography or segment of business.

An example in which such access was a market need is the Austrian Post's creation of value-added delivery by offering one-stop-shop solutions for their customers, including procurement, fulfilment and delivery. They also looked far beyond letters and parcels, considering everything from televisions to coffee[5]. One of its customers is the online food service KochAbo.at, which offers online grocery shopping. Home grocery delivery is an emerging market and one with exponential potential as customers seek time savers for their over-packed professional and personal schedules.

The Austrian Post provides procurement services for KochAbo.at by receiving delivery of high-quality fresh food from local companies at a warehouse in Vienna in the early morning. The Post also provides fulfilment services, including picking and packaging, which includes EPP boxes, cooling packs and special thermo packaging for long-distance delivery to clients all over Austria. The Post is delivering up to 1,000 KochAbo.at deliveries per day, including same-day delivery in capital cities and next-day delivery via overnight service[6].

What would it be like for your organisation to behave like a new entrant in the market by providing new services, such as home grocery delivery or fulfilment services for online retailers? Or what about competing with e-retailers and traditional retail by offering an online storefront for multiple small businesses and providing their fulfilment services?

---

5   'Behind the Scenes: E-fulfillment Warehouses', 2014 presentation by Gerald Gregori, Senior Vice President Logistics Services, Parcel & Logistics, Austrian Post

6   Ibid.

How will you take the assets that you have today and evolve them to give your customers the experience they desire tomorrow?

CONCLUSION

Every successful company has an 'est', something that they are best at. They are the fastest, easiest, largest, simplest or just, plainly, best at something they do. You must find out what you can be best at. What is your differentiation? This focus on the est is how many successful organisations find their niche and create differentiation. This can also be a starting place for identifying your focus markets. Finding out what you are best at and who values that offering are two of the fundamental steps to create effective market segmentation. From that point, you can start to understand the value generated and how your organisation can exploit the opportunity to become the best, most-valued provider in your new-found niche. This is how we separate out what our customers want – that for which they are ultimately willing to pay a premium – from what they need. Zappos.com didn't set out to become a returns company, but when they realised that their est, according to their customers, was their unique returns policy, they leveraged that to act like a new entrant in the increasingly crowded shoe e-retailer market. Listening to your customers, determining who they are and what experience they desire, can provide significant insight on how you can determine what your best is. You can then use this to behave like a new entrant in the market.

QUESTION FOR THOUGHT AND DISCUSSION

How will you take the assets that you have today and evolve them to give your customers the experience they desire tomorrow?

Direct mail is increasingly seen as one of the largest components of the data-driven marketing economy.

CHANGING MARKETS, CHANGING MARKETING: THE OUTLOOK FOR IMPROVING ADVERTISING MAIL

Laraine Balk Hope and Jean Philippe Ducasse*

United States Postal Service Office of the Inspector General

INTRODUCTION

Advertising is critical to commerce around the world – and direct mail, also known as advertising mail ('admail'), has an important place among marketing channels. Direct mail is both a stand-alone marketing channel and, increasingly, complementary to other channels, especially those enabled through digital communications and other advances in technology. Some aspects of digital communications, such as personalisation and micro-targeting, can be incorporated into new hard-copy mail strategies. Such efforts, along with integrating direct mail into other marketing channels, will allow mail recipients greater choice in their ordering and feedback channels. These developments are likely to ensure a solid place for direct mail among advertising vehicles in both the near- and longer-term.

MAIL REMAINS A KEY ELEMENT OF THE AD MIX

As the global economy has been improving, direct mail is slowly recovering. In the United States, Winterberry predicts that direct-mail spending will grow 1.1% in

---

* NOTE: The views presented here are those of the authors and do not necessarily represent those of the Office of the Inspector General, US Postal Service, or any other organisation.

2014 to $ 44.5 billion (vs. $ 50.1 billion for digital).[1] Admail still holds a solid 13% share of total advertising expenditure; the same as in 2008. It represents 43% of all US retail advertising and is still the single largest local media channel.

In the United Kingdom, where digital advertising revenue overtook direct mail as far back as 2007, direct mail now represents 10% of the total spent. After losing share to these 'newer' advertising methods, direct mail is being adapted to a new role as one of the major data-driven media. In fact, PricewaterhouseCoopers, in its ten-year outlook through 2023, expects UK admail volumes to stabilise at their current levels as digital media progressively mature (see Figure 1, below). Other direct mail-intensive countries are expected to follow the same pattern.

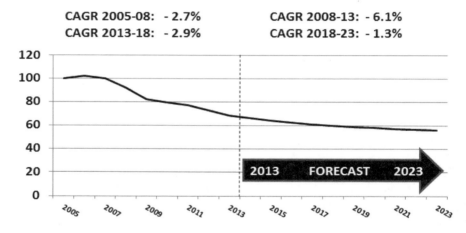

Figure 1: United Kingdom direct mail historical and projected volumes 2005–2023, indexed mail volumes (2005=100)[2]

DIRECT MAIL'S STRATEGIC IMPORTANCE FOR POSTS IS INCREASING

In the US, most hard-copy advertisements, coupons and non-profit solicitations are sent via the Standard Mail class, formerly known as Third-Class Mail.[3] Standard

---

1   *Winterberry Group*, '2014 Annual Outlook: What to Expect in Direct and Digital Marketing', 9 January 2014

2   PricewaterhouseCoopers (PwC), 'The Outlook for UK Mail Volumes to 2023', July 2013, based on Royal Mail data and PwC analysis

3   Standard Mail was known as Third-Class Mail until 1996.

Mail accounts for about half of total mail volume, or 80 billion out of 158 billion pieces.[4] In FY 2013, Standard Mail generated about $17 billion in revenues for the USPS and, as a mature product, is more important than ever, in the light of declines in First-Class Mail correspondence and transactional mail.

This growing importance of direct mail is shared by many countries, albeit to a lesser extent than in the US. In Australia for instance, the share of direct mail letters has increased from 12% in 2004 to 17% in 2012.[5] However, due in large part to there being more overall mail volume per capita, direct mail intensity in the United States remains significantly higher than in any other nation.[6]

COMBINING TRADITIONAL AND NEW APPROACHES
UNITED STATES

Ironically, given today's emphasis on personalisation and targeting, the creation of Third-Class Mail enabled bulk mailings to reach recipients cheaply, with standardised messages and less privacy protection than First-Class Mail. (Initially, Third-Class Mailings were required to be unsealed.) The USPS started offering discounts to mailers for presorted bulk Third-Class Mail in 1979, and subsequently developed different pricing tiers, based on presort level, method of preparation and other requirements. Discounts for drop shipping (inducting bulk mail into the mailstream closer to destination) soon followed. Later, geographic segmentation by postal carrier route was enabled, with even lower postage rates. This helped local businesses and drove the growth of 'neighbourhood mail' (combinations of coupons and offerings from local merchants together in one envelope), often managed by large national corporations.

Standard Mail, however, long ago ceased to be a 'one size fits all' vehicle; today, even neighbourhood mailings are often customised by household through use of complex algorithms and variable data printing technology. As recently as ten years

---

4   The number of pieces of Standard Mail in the US is approximately the same as that of the entire letter market in Europe.

5   According to the UPU postal statistics (available from: http://www.upu.int/en/resources/postal-statistics/query-the-database.html). Mail class differentiations and accompanying taxonomy vary from country to country. While most posts have specific direct-mail products, access conditions (such as contents or minimum volumes), addressing and preparation requirements vary considerably across countries. Many items classified as 'unaddressed' in Europe or Canada are considered 'addressed' in the United States, owing to the Postal Service's mailbox monopoly.

6   The number of addressed admail pieces per delivery point per year is 559 in the United States, vs 129 in France, 118 in Germany, 84 in Canada and 38 in Italy (Source: IPC, Presentation to the UPU DMAB, April 2013).

ago, some niche postal product offerings, such as Customised Market Mail (CMM), were considered extremely creative and cutting edge. CMM allowed mailers to send direct mail in shapes other than rectangular, with cut-outs which had previously been prohibited.

What constitutes 'cutting edge' has changed dramatically over the last decade. While traditional direct mail exists and is successful, product development now emphasises enhancements that more directly involve the mail recipient and tie to digital communications in one form or another. For example, the USPS has recently offered promotions and discounts for mailpieces that include Quick Response (QR) codes, links to Augmented Reality (AR) and even Near Field Communication (NFC), which is considered to be quickly increasing in importance. The USPS is offering a total of seven direct-mail promotions in 2014, including promotions to encourage mailers 'buying up' to First-Class Mail.

Major printers have led the way in developing new ways to enhance digital-print options, allowing communication to be interactive between advertiser and mail recipient. Printers are combining various digital technologies with print on paper while building their overall creative and quantitative capabilities to both (1) handle 'big data' analytics and (2) assist advertisers in personalising campaigns by content and channel. One senior executive from a leading printer observed that when his firm first entered the interactive digital-print arena, everyone thought there would be a clear technology replacement cycle – for example, when QR died, AR would take over, then NFC, and so forth. However, the company learned quickly that each type of technology has unique strengths and weaknesses; it is best to offer customers multiple technologies, so that they can offer mail recipients exactly what they want, when they want it, from a variety of channel choices. Since technology is evolving so rapidly, flexibility is key.

INTERNATIONAL PERSPECTIVES

Postal operators across the globe are embracing similar best practices and often reaching similar conclusions, although implementation strategies may vary.

La Poste (France), among others, launched a 'connected mail' service in 2012 – a one-stop shopping solution whereby the post provides business mailers with QR codes and mobile microsites dedicated to their campaign.[7] China Post has

---

7   http://www.laposte.fr/Entreprise/Marketing-Direct/Les-solutions/Conception-des-documents/Conception-documents/Concevoir-une-communication-creative-et-originale/Courrier-connecte-site-mobile

established specialised advertising agencies to help mailers efficiently combine direct mail with other advertising channels, including newspapers and outdoor LED display ads.[8] Swiss Post (SPS) offers Customer Relationship Management (CRM) and loyalty programs that enable omni-channel processes and help craft more targeted messages.[9]

Postal operators also create omni-channel experiences for recipients. For example, PostNL's Spotta platform gives recipients access to advertising leaflets, which are delivered in paper format by the Dutch Post or accessed through a mobile app.[10]

'BIG DATA' ANALYTICS PRESENT POTENTIAL OPPORTUNITIES AND PITFALLS

'Big data' is a colloquial term for large, unstructured datasets combined with powerful analytics. Big data enables marketers to amass more intelligence from varied sources. The long-established use of personally identifiable information (such as names and postal addresses) for targeted marketing purposes is increasingly being complemented by aggregated and anonymised big data – with a focus on improving ad effectiveness. This is possible through better targeting and increased efficiency, with more economical media buying.[11]

For instance, the application of analytics to tweets, social networks, blogs or websites can, in addition to ordering patterns, provide insights on customers' sentiment: their reactions to a direct-mail campaign, new products or their expectations of a new service.

CUSTOMISING THE 'INTERNET OF POSTAL THINGS' TO HELP CUSTOMERS

Posts are among the largest 'producers' of big data, even if that data is not currently accessed on a regular basis. Scans of letter mail pieces along the processing chain create terabytes of new data every day, which can potentially increase the value of

---

8   'China Post Expands its Direct Marketing Development through Big Data,' China Direct Mail Association presentation to the UPU DMAB, 1 April 2014

9   http://www.swisspost.ch/post-startseite/post-geschaeftskunden/post-dokumente-dialog-loesungen/post-customer-relationship-excellence/post-crm-loyalty-marketing.htm

10   http://www.spotta.nl/organisatie/over-spotta

11   http://www.iab.net/media/file/FromInformatonToAudiences-AWinterberryGroupWhite Paper-January2012.pdf

direct mail for mailers and recipients.[12] All components of the postal infrastructure can now become the source of new types of mass data, whether sensor data from connected vehicles or letter boxes, or information generated by letter carriers: this is what is called the 'Internet of Postal Things'. Posts are increasingly equipping carriers with handheld terminals. This provides a potential opportunity to capture more information at the doorstep.

Although they have access to mega data, posts recognise they are not yet data-driven organisations. As posts start to experiment with big data, it is not yet clear how far they will go. The cost of collecting data is declining, but the sheer effort required to clean, analyse and share findings is daunting. Furthermore, few postal operators know how to combine the data management and marketing skills needed to take advantage of 'postal big data'. The postal learning journey is just starting and the outlook for direct mail is exciting.

As a March 2014 Australia Post study stated, 'the migration of eyeballs from traditional to digital is myth.'[13] Although fewer mailings are sent, these mailings increasingly stand out and are widely read and acted upon. Demographic trends also help keep direct mail in vogue: a recent study in the US confirmed that Millennials like and use direct mail, if appropriately targeted. (While it is a truism to state that people want targeted mail, Millennials are even more unhappy with unwanted direct mail than older demographic groups[14].) As part of this mission, posts can help to enable a feedback loop so that advertisers have better information on what customers want.

Contrary to the popular theories championing an 'omni-channel' strategy for all customers, a more pragmatic approach to direct mail and other media is to offer different choices to different people. Both messages and media can be tailored by customer: not every customer needs to engage in every experience. Just as the message that advertisers send to their target readerships is critically important, so too is whether the message is: (1) a unique communication or (2) part of a

---

12 For example, La Poste is testing a program to share data with households on the number and type of mail pieces they have received. This information could be used as a basis for more targeted mailings – letting customers receive more of the type of direct-mail pieces they want and opt out of the type of direct-mail pieces they are not interested in.

13 http://auspost.com.au/business-solutions/research-oct13-brands.html

14 United States Postal Service Office of the Inspector General white paper, RARC-WP-14-001, 'Enhancing Mail for Digital Natives', 18 November 2013, available from: http://www.uspsoig.gov/story/risk-analysis-research-center-papers/enhancing-mail-digital-natives

more complex and ongoing multimedia strategy. If the latter, the strategy should encourage customers to provide feedback to advertisers on what they want and need, in an environment respecting and protecting privacy. Flexibility and the ability to adapt between messaging platforms are essential.

IMPORTANCE OF PRIVACY

For many years, some countries have had strictly enforced privacy laws that limit the use of personal information, in particular for marketing purposes.[15] A proposed EU regulation and a proposed directive set a framework for data protection aimed at strengthening online privacy rights and reinforcing users' confidence.[16] In the US, the direct-marketing industry encourages a responsible use of data by marketers. Whether or not mandated or enforced by statute, guarding personal information is a prerequisite for the long-term sustainability of direct-mail business as part of the fast-growing data-driven economy. Postal operators who have not already done so will also need to develop clear data transparency and privacy policies dealing with questions such as: who owns the information collected? whose permission is needed to collect it? and under what forms and conditions will it be disseminated?[17]

CONCLUSION

In just a few years, the US and global perspective on direct mail has changed radically. When it comes to engaging customers, the long-standing 'paper vs digital' alternative is losing relevance. Direct mail is increasingly seen as one of the largest components of the data-driven marketing economy. And, notably, the trend toward more specialisation in advertising promotions ('niching down', as one US-industry observer called it) is picking up. This is possible through clever and competent use of big-data analytics.

As trusted stewards of personal information and as providers of new data sets that potentially add value to mail, posts can participate in the paradigm change, helping direct mail become (or continue to be) one of the most effective, efficient and innovative marketing channels for the next decade and beyond.

---

15 For example, France has had such laws in effect since 1978.

16 For an update on the EU data protection reform, see http://europa.eu/rapid/press-release_ MEMO-14-60_en.htm.

17 See International Postal Big Data: Discussion Forum Recap, USPS OIG, May 2014, available from: https://www.uspsoig.gov/sites/default/files/document-library-files/2014/rarc-ib-14-002. pdf

QUESTION FOR THOUGHT AND DISCUSSION

How can posts better integrate their hard-copy and digital offerings with strategies that require quick adaptation to new channels of communication?

As competition in the B2C parcel-delivery sector increases, success will be decided based on the price, quality, services and features offered both to the sender and the receiver.

THE CHANGING MARKET: 'POSTAL' BECOMING 'LOGISTICS'?

Erwin Lenhardt

T-Systems

INTRODUCTION

Companies and organisations involved in postal and delivery services are undergoing profound transformation. The paradigm shift towards digitisation, with an increasingly mobile population and rapid growth in worldwide e-commerce, means that the industry faces completely new challenges. Many key technologies are capable of supporting and even shaping this change and of achieving greater logistical efficiency in the course of modernisation.

POSTAL DIVERSIFICATION

The Thurn and Taxis dynasty is said to have initiated the idea of a postal service for reliable transport and delivery of mail as early as the fifteenth century. Since then, postal services have been established in every country for transport and delivery of mail. As paper has been the predominant medium of communication, letter mail has been the main business of postal services for most of this time. By contrast, 'cargo', the transportation of goods, has traditionally been handled by freight forwarders, railways and trucking companies.

Up to the end of the last century, the key drivers of business growth were the growing demand for paper-based communication and the increased capability of postal services for fast and reliable delivery. Parcels played a minor role. With electronic communication starting to take over in business communication by the 1990s, early adopters within the postal community saw parcel and freight logistics as one of the most important areas of diversification. The acquisition of DHL by Deutsche Post and TNT by the Dutch Post were important landmarks in this trend.

Since the beginning of the century, the decline in the volume of letters has been accepted as an industry trend and the revival of parcel business, in addition to other ideas for diversification, has become a 'must' for postal services – as has the making of further inroads into the transport logistics business. For some operators, the revival of parcel business was accompanied by entry into 'logistics fulfilment', third-party logistics and transport logistics for pallets and containers. This was often achieved through organic growth and acquisitions.

E-COMMERCE DRIVING PARCEL LOGISTICS

With online purchasing playing an increasing role in consumer shopping behaviour and having overcome the global financial crisis of 2009–2010, e-commerce has become the driving force for parcel logistics. Many operators are experiencing almost double-digit parcel-traffic growth rates. With B2B (business to business) parcel traffic growing with expanding international trade at single-digit growth rates, domestic B2C (business to consumer) parcel-delivery growth currently dominates the logistics industry. With various initiatives to facilitate international e-commerce, B2C parcel logistics will become more and more internationalised, further stimulating the e-commerce parcel market.

Growing parcel traffic attracts competitors, often resulting in the deterioration of profit margins, and thus a strong need for increased efficiency in parcel operations and for new ways of differentiation. In addition, large e-commerce traders like OTTO in Germany, Amazon in the US and 360-Buy in China have started their own parcel-delivery operations. The battle for market share in the growing parcel-logistics market is on, with great prospects for those operators who can stay ahead.

LONG-TERM GROWTH FOR B2B LOGISTICS

B2B logistics is closely linked with the economic business cycle which now is in an underlying long-term upward trend, backed by growing international trade due to globalisation. The industry has seen continued standardisation of shipping units (containers, parcel and pallets) and services as well as improved quality of delivery. In this context, operators need other points of competitive difference to stay ahead in order to avoid competing solely on price. Differentiation will be achieved by offering value-added services in the area of physical-goods handling and in the capture and management of data associated with the goods and their transport.

SAME-DAY LOGISTICS

The ability to order goods online that are not otherwise universally available and the existence of convenient parcel-delivery services are now allowing purchases that previously, without the Internet, would not have been possible. This has also led consumers to bypass local stores for goods 'available cheaper elsewhere'. Furthermore, e-commerce dealers are now starting to offer food and grocery services.

Established retailers have realised that they need to fight back in order not to lose market share to e-commerce traders. For this reason, traditional retail chains are also starting to offer home-delivery services from regional distribution centres.

Both trends create a need for 'same-day delivery logistics', an operation that needs a high level of support from real-time management information with regard to customers, goods, traffic and environmental conditions. Currently, same-day logistics services are being market tested by operators from various backgrounds. Do such operations also represent a profitable opportunity for postal services?

LOGISTICS IT – THE KEY TO SUCCESS FOR B2B LOGISTICS!

Manufacturing and retail industries are under constant pressure to align more strongly and optimise the total supply chain, for which the availability of relevant and timely information is critical. With globally distributed value chains, B2B logistics needs to be able to deliver speedily, reliably and on time. Furthermore, logistics operators need to be able to provide much more information to the customer's supply-chain management system about the status of goods. The need for more data about the status of goods in transit requires intelligent censoring, communication and IT systems that are able to aggregate and supply information to the various stakeholders within the supply chain.

The automotive industry, a sector most experienced with distributed and closely linked supply chains, is taking the lead in requiring and implementing a new generation of transportation logistics information systems. Other industries are following. Eventually, transport logistics providers will have to offer these kinds of sophisticated information platforms to stay ahead. Logistics operators have choices: invest in their own next-generation transport IT system, join a shared service transport IT platform, or team up with a transport IT provider to create a leading-edge joint transport IT service for their logistics customer.

One example of innovative transport logistics is 'Bag2Go'. This 'talking' case was developed by an aircraft manufacturer in association with T-Systems and a case manufacturer. The case is equipped with a mobile-phone chip and constantly reports its location to the owner using RFID and GPS. When fully established, this innovative technology will allow transport of baggage to be completely independent of the traveller. In an analogous application in the field of B2B logistics, the Bag2Go concept could be adapted to a Parcel2Go, thus realising a value-added service that would deliver valuable additional benefits to both sender and receiver. For example, the delivery of urgently needed spare parts for production machines could be made much more efficient and transparent.

LOGISTICS IT – THE KEY TO SUCCESS FOR B2C LOGISTICS!

As competition in the B2C parcel-delivery sector increases, success will be decided based on the price, quality, services and features offered both to the sender *and* the receiver.

A current focus for the end-customer segment is the 'last mile'. This is not only because the cost from the last transfer point to the receiver's home is normally higher than all previous costs, but also because the receiver's preferences and habits play an equally important role. The logistics operator is faced with the choice of running the risk that the receiver is not at home or communicating with the receiver to make an appointment and then having to re-plan a corresponding route. A promising solution to this problem is found in already-well-established app technology. A mobile app on a smartphone allows the receiver and logistics operator quickly and easily to reach agreement on delivery.

The receiver's choice about 'when and where' the delivery is to take place and convenient interaction between the sender and operator will be major differentiating factors for parcel operators. As the usage of smartphones and tablet PCs increases, receivers' interaction will be based on mobile app services. Last-mile IT solutions for interaction with receivers need to be closely interlinked in real time with last-mile parcel handling and transport management systems. The ability to provide flexibility and maximum convenience for receivers will decide the receiver's parcel-logistics operator preference.

Last-mile logistics IT solutions will therefore play an important role in increasing parcel-operator efficiency, with operators who provide such solutions being preferred by receivers. Logistics IT systems will thus be a key success factor for B2C parcel-logistics operators.

NEW BUSINESS MODELS FOR LOGISTICS IT APPLICATIONS

Traditionally, logistics IT solutions were proprietary systems implemented as part of an operator's network-infrastructure development project. With IT solutions playing a greater role in operator competitiveness, there will be more pressure on implementation and continuous improvement of these systems, requiring shorter implementation times and shorter technology refresh cycles. IT solution providers are preparing for standardised logistics IT products that allow for faster implementation through customisation and easier maintenance and upgrade. Also, dedicated logistics IT solution providers are expected to offer shared customised use of cloud-based solutions. Cloud-based 'logistics IT as a service' will provide greater flexibility to logistics operators to deploy more rapidly and use logistics IT solutions in their network infrastructure.

CONCLUSION

Logistics provides a vital opportunity for diversification for postal operators. However, market growth and increasing standardisation require optimisation and differentiation. Logistics IT solutions not only enable great improvements in operational efficiency but can also provide differentiation. Logistics operators need to place greater emphasis on the value of logistics IT systems, IT implementation and utilisation. Operators will be able to choose between the implementation of a tailor-made proprietary IT solution or standardised logistics IT platforms. There will also be cloud-based logistics IT solutions as a service offered by key IT players, giving operators even greater choice in utilising the benefits of modern logistics IT applications. Cloud services have the particular benefit of allowing response to fluctuations in workload – such as seasonal demand peaks – without driving up fixed costs for IT. Operators will need to review market developments in logistics IT and make the right choice to support their dynamic businesses.

QUESTION FOR THOUGHT AND DISCUSSION

It is argued here that using real-time information from senders and receivers through a logistics IT platform will be a key differentiator between operators and will be essential in order to compete for B2B and B2C parcel business. What are the operational implications for postal companies in terms of real-time decision making, planning and resource optimisation?

SECTION 2
CHANGING THE WAY POSTS ARE LED

Derek Osborn

In the context of the changing market and with an industry in the midst of transformation, *exceptional leadership* is clearly essential for companies or businesses which aim not just to survive but to thrive. However, the postal sector is currently in uncharted waters, making the task of leadership even more difficult and daunting – but even more important – now that the horizons are obscure and the short-term prospects stormy!

Maurizio Puppo discusses what kind of leadership the industry needs today, especially when the direction and destination are unclear. He uses the example of Christopher Columbus, who was not a textbook leader but nevertheless made some extraordinary and surprising 'accidental' discoveries through serendipity. In this way, he illustrates that some of the characteristics needed for leaders today may be courage, imagination and the ability to inspire.

Janras Kotsi has a lifetime of experience of leadership in the South African Post Office. Against the backdrop of incredible transformation and change in both the country and the mail industry, he charts the transformational journey that the company embarked on. He outlines how and why they set out to make radical changes and then openly shares their experiences and what they learnt in the process. As with all such ventures, there were both successes and lessons learnt, especially about developing collective leadership and gaining commitment at all levels.

Shailendra Dwivedi approaches the postal leadership challenge more broadly, describing the need (and opportunity) for posts to be in the centre of (and lead) the new economy, potentially as the central network of networks, connecting physical, electronic and financial platforms. This requires much more collective and collaborative behaviour and attitudes from leaders, rather than the traditional monopoly or tribal thinking that only focuses on its own goals and objectives.

Building on this theme of taking wider responsibility and the idea that 'no business is an island', **Liene Norberg** and I connect postal leadership with the broader sustainability challenges that face all sectors and indeed everyone on the planet. We discuss the outcome of a recent benchmarking workshop and survey on the strategic leadership challenges relating to sustainability. There are significant opportunities here for the postal industry and all its stakeholders to take a strong lead.

'If one does not know to which port one is sailing, no wind is favourable.'

WHAT KIND OF LEADERSHIP DOES THE POSTAL INDUSTRY NEED TODAY?

Maurizio Puppo

Solystic

INTRODUCTION

'If one does not know to which port one is sailing, no wind is favourable'. This much-quoted line of Seneca seems to suggest that the most important quality of an effective leader is simply 'knowing where to go'. It is hard, at first glance, to disagree with that. The first reaction could be to deploy a classical management planning process: (1) as Seneca said, know exactly where you want to go – decide your strategic goals (good!); (2) investigate the feasibility and identify the means of achieving those goals (perfect!); (3) monitor progress towards the fulfilment of these objectives, with regard to remedial actions where necessary (needless to say!)... All of this, of course, is taken directly from the handbook of the perfect manager.

SERENDIPITY

I am very sorry, but let me stop there. Fortunately, reality (as well as the Roman philosopher's thought) is not quite as black and white, nor so straightforward. A good manager will be likely to follow these steps and will be right to do so. But a leader is arguably something different from a good manager.

One of the hardest English words to translate into other languages is 'serendipity'. If you look for its definition, you will find something like a 'fortuitous happenstance' or 'pleasant surprise'. In other words, you could say it is finding something valuable or delightful when you were not actually looking for it. The history of my fellow citizen Christopher Columbus is a good example of serendipity. Columbus based his calculations on dramatically incorrect assumptions about the size of the earth. He assumed that it would be feasible to reach eastern Asia ('the Indies') by sailing approximately 3,000 miles west. Technically speaking (and compared with current theories of planning and management), this was an enormous mistake.

WAS HE A GOOD LEADER?

If we take seriously the sentence of Seneca, we cannot but note that Christopher Columbus did not know to which port he was sailing. His strategic goal was fuzzy and vague: 'the Indies'. From this perspective, his journey was a circuitous trip into the absolute unknown.

As for investigating the feasibility and the means of achieving his objectives, his approach was based on completely wrong assumptions and dramatically inadequate. The distance from Europe to Japan is much bigger than Columbus expected and it would have been impossible for a ship of the fifteenth century to carry enough food and fresh water for such a journey.

Let us now turn to his monitoring of progress. Despite his mistaken calculation and the unforeseen presence of a continent between Europe and eastern Asia, the trip was much longer than anticipated by either Columbus or his crew. So, in order to avoid the apprehensions of the crew, Columbus kept two sets of logs. The first one, which he kept totally secret, showed the truth (the real distance travelled each day). The other was false and under-reported the true distance travelled from their homeland. This was a classic case of problem hiding: the issues are hidden from governance until it is too late to take any corrective action (such as, for example, immediately turning back in order to avoid dying in the ocean).

Let's face it: from the point of view of the handbook of the perfect manager, Columbus's attitude was a total, absolute disaster. His plan could be regarded as a perfect example of the stupidity of a small-minded strategist. Fuzzy goals, complacency and superficiality, an ability to lie and manipulate, a tendency to hide or downplay problems…

THE RESULT?

However, everybody knows the consequence of this stupidity and this bad, ineffective management. Columbus did not reach his fuzzy, vague goal, 'the Indies'; he landed on the Caribbean islands and thus 'discovered', for European people, the American continents. This was a historic event that changed the history of the world, both for good and for bad (because, you remember, reality is never quite as black and white, nor so straightforward...).

CONCLUSION

Compared with the requirements of modern management theory as found in textbooks, Columbus was definitely a bad manager; but nevertheless, he was also a shining light as an inspirational leader, able to lead his crew to an unknown destination. There should be no confusion between the natures of these two roles. When there is a need for a deep change, you will need leaders as well as good managers.

This is the case in the postal industry today, whose business model was not built for the dramatic changes currently reshaping it, such as the rise of the Internet, electronic payments and alternative delivery methods. If the *status quo* is not sustainable, which seems likely, the postal industry needs leaders both able to imagine where they would like to go and brave enough to set sail, even if they don't yet know exactly to which port they will be sailing, nor what they will become. 'If one does not know to which port one is sailing, no wind is favourable': instead of standing still, a real leader will try to imagine where the port could be, and will sail towards it and an unknown future.

QUESTION FOR THOUGHT AND DISCUSSION

Do we have these kinds of brave and inspirational leaders in the postal industry today? If not, where are we to find them and how should the job description read?

Arguably, leadership was the differentiating factor between survival and annihilation.

LEADERSHIP NEEDED TO DRIVE CHANGE IN THE MODERN POSTAL WORLD

Janras Kotsi

South African Post Office

INTRODUCTION

What do you do when throwing money at problems no longer works – moreover, when there is no money to throw? This is a challenge faced by many formerly lucrative industries when confronted by disruptive innovation. Numerous enterprises have felt the wrath of change in the past century as whole industries lost relevance. It is interesting to note that some companies come out of such conditions stronger, while many are relegated to the dustbin of history. Arguably, leadership was the differentiating factor between survival and annihilation. Enterprises in the postal industry are now at their own crossroads.

Currently, the postal industry is facing bombardment with disruptive innovation – innovation that is driven by changes in the market, shifting value propositions, new generations of customers, evolving technology, novel arrangements of supply chains and 'sneaky' competition that has often worked out how to evade regulations and stay relevant. In essence, this poses a big question: what kind of leadership is needed to drive successful change in the modern postal world? In 2008, this leadership challenge arrived in the South African Post Office.

A BURNING PLATFORM FOR SOUTH AFRICA

The challenges facing our leadership were no different to those in the rest of the postal industry. Letter volumes were declining for the first time in our history. This decline was due to different factors including: electronic substitutions; extraterritorial offices entering our markets; the regulators' maturity in enforcing our compliance whilst being less able to enforce the compliance of our competitors (so that they encroached on the reserved market area); dramatic restructuring of government subsidies; and moreover, the universal service obligation remaining in force.

Universal service meant that further investment was needed in the logistics infrastructure to enable all citizens to access postal services. Urban residential areas were rapidly developing and there was a vast underserviced rural population. This resulted in overcapacity, high costs and stagnant revenue. In the midst of all this, letters represented the main source of revenue for the mail business, whilst mail business was two-thirds of the South African Post Office. These external factors were compounded by internal culture and attitudes.

Internally, there was a growing view that mail was dead and thus that any voluntary investment would be fruitless. In addition, the mail business had an aging staff, often with capabilities that were a mismatch for the knowledge economy. Our executives and the whole workforce had a competency set suitable for the industrial age, which was focused on processes and compliance. We were still celebrating the heroes of the previous transition from the bureaucratic culture of the public service to our current process-driven organisation. We were not ready for this era, which demands a commercially savvy workforce. We had to develop a response to this dilemma.

CASE FOR CHANGE

The mail business could not afford to respond to this predicament using the prevailing paradigm. The prevailing paradigm was to throw technology, process optimisation and systems enhancement into sustaining existing products. We had already received numerous national and international accolades for using cutting-edge technologies such as biometrics, RFid and robust enterprise resource planning. We had adopted a number of systems endorsed by the Universal Postal Union. We could do more things, but doing things was not enough. We realised that our main priority was that we had to improve our ability to lead people.

The mail business needed a high-calibre leadership that could overhaul the philosophy, paradigm, processes and practices of conducting its business. The journey ahead of us demanded collective leadership more than a leader, and this could only be forged by a rigorous methodology rather than uncoordinated events.

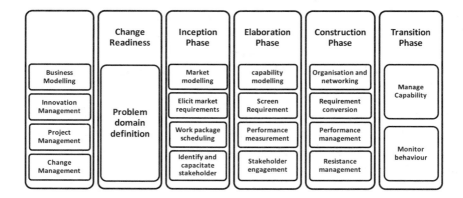

Figure 1: Mail-business transformation roadmap

Our choice of methodology (Figure 1) highlighted that collective leadership is initiated through comprehension of the common threat, elevated by a change-vision advocacy and sustained by the development of strategy; only then would work begin on technology or products. Advocating a change vision provided a platform for internalisation of the transformation journey by the collective leadership of our executive team. In the mail business, we explored and experienced these Kotter Model first steps.

CREATING AN ORGANISATIONAL CLIMATE

We quickly learned that strategy is a complex science and sophisticated art, which is underpinned by relationships that act as its centre of gravity. The leader in the modern postal world must be competent in the art of relationships and the science of forceful execution. The relationship starts at the executive team level.

The executive team must be given a reason to lead change and that reason must be anchored on the immediate and compelling threat. The mail business had that compelling threat in the form of electronic substitution, which was eating into letter volumes, and meagre parcel growth that was not replacing the lost revenue; whilst simultaneously, the cost drivers were pushing upwards.

Our subordinates indicated that, as an executive team, we were not visible. They felt that our strategy was unfocussed and further observed that our administrative tempo made us incapable of mounting any sustainable innovation programme. Moreover, the executives had their grievances about being delegated responsibility without receiving the corresponding authority. There was an urgent need for change.

Change occurs at an individual level before it takes shape at team level (see Figure 2) and, consequently, some primary stumbling blocks are personal risk perceptions and grievances. The leader in the modern postal world needs to be transparent and able to reassure others that the transformation journey is not inspired by a hidden agenda. To achieve this, the executive team assembled an internal support team that drew its competencies from the fields of social science, engineering and commerce.

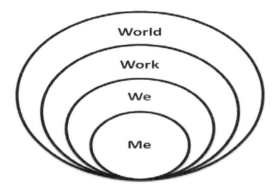

Figure 2: SAPO transformation framework

The support team was there to provide technical backup on change. It had to design appropriate frameworks to be used, such as maps and rules of engagement for our journey, and recommend them to the collective leadership. These frameworks had to be based on scientifically tested methodologies and they had to be simple in order to be driven by our executive team with internal support and minimal external intervention – which was only involved to escalate the robustness of the engagements, help resolve unspoken relationships which were straining matters and provide international trends.

After two years of consistent focus on the executive team, the climate remained tense. The case for change and the frameworks remained something to which lip service was paid, but they had not been internalised. The awareness was high and correct words were used, but the behaviours remained the same.

PERSONAL JOURNEY

The lack of desire that was displayed could easily have shaken our conviction and compelled us to change our maps. However, we chose to forge ahead and take the next step on our journey. We knew from our analysis that trust shown by a leader sponsoring a change can create wonders. We displayed that trust by handing over responsibility to executives to advocate the change vision in their divisions and further assigned them to particular geographic areas. This was despite the fact that their own buy-in was questionable.

In this way, the mail business was able to 'shock' the system and the executives realised that they were not ready to advocate the change vision. The change in dynamics enriched relationships between executives and their support teams. Moreover, the mandate was very clear: to get a commitment from the second layer of leadership. The executives were to engage and capacitate the second layer of leadership on the case for change. Initially, they went through the motions, completed the tick sheet and complained about a lack of real action. The glossy reports were compiled. There was no proper coaching.

Coaching is a fundamental reinforcement tool for a leader in the modern postal world. Trust is sustained through conscious reinforcement. The relevant reinforcement in our case was coaching anchored by the impact-assessment results. It reflected the quality of second layer of commitment. Initially, negative results created a platform for crucial confrontation on the conceptualisation of the mandate and frameworks. Then, coaching from the primary sponsor of change and assigned support-team members became a necessity. Moreover, the results created the desire to get a proper commitment from their constituency, thus pushing the executives to enter their personal journey.

Entering one's personal journey can be a vulnerable time, which may result in more disengagement. We witnessed resignations and withdrawal symptoms from our executive team. In other cases, the personal journey actually triggered more commitment, which had eluded the team for two years. We were consistent in our resolve to insist on devotion to the vision and frameworks, whilst providing coaching and other support. Hence, the leader in the modern postal world must have a compelling change vision and then coach on it rather than depend upon command and control. Coaching helps individuals to deal with consistent environmental changes. The right climate at executive level set an appropriate platform to develop a strategy to navigate modern market conditions.

STRATEGY CO-CREATION

Strategy development in the modern postal world has to be a co-creation of the executive team rather than being formulated by a brilliant external professional. Moreover, the leader must maximise the use of all the experience in the organisation, beyond just the executive team, to develop a credible and evolving strategy. After three years in this transformation journey, we started reformulating it, expanding from its 'need for change' theme to design a fresh business model and define a full project portfolio (Figure 3). Further, we resourced our programme by empowering our people for broader action.

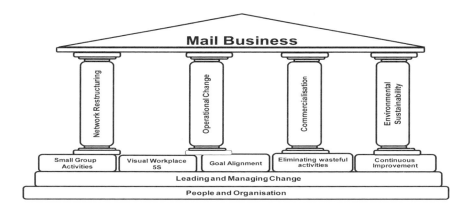

Figure 3: Mail business strategy pillars

The empowerment of the second layer of leadership increased the number of 'change mandate' holders in order to engage commitment in the third layer of leadership. This brought more internal partners into the scheme of strategy co-creation. Consequently, there was a rise in the quality of strategy engagement, business-model comprehension and programme rollout. As a result, we have seen greater adoption of the strategy direction and better utilisation of frameworks – although we must admit that proficiency in our frameworks remains low. Nevertheless, we are increasingly witnessing the strategy coming to life in line with our transformation journey theme.

CELEBRATING THE GAINS

A leader in the modern postal world must also celebrate the wins. We are already reaping fruits by moving from commanding towards coaching, anchored on impact evaluation. Due to our approach, the mail business is celebrating certification of its quality-management system compliance with international standards, namely the ISO 9001, during the fourth year of our transformation journey. The scope for the South African Bureau of Standards (SABS) audit covered four hundred and twenty two sites with fourteen thousand staff.

The mail business is also meeting its environmental sustainability targets. We are reducing our carbon emissions and energy usage, and recycling more material. The environmental indicators were voluntarily subjected to international standards and we are part of the sustainability programme of the International Postal Corporation (IPC). A change leader must also subject his or her performance to external verification and validation.

We have also boosted our quality-management system by the introduction of lean management. This formalisation of our continuous improvement program is our tactical approach to enable us to exceed our customer expectations. We are sure that the fifth year of transformation will close with a celebration of the success of this initiative. We will then focus on the commercial aptitude of the whole workforce, whilst reconfiguring our logistics network.

REFLECTIONS – WHAT HAVE WE LEARNT?

We have to upgrade our proficiency in applying frameworks. As much as work is progressing, we remain concerned about the acceptance of roles and responsibilities. The level of commitment remains fragile, which is the consequence of the deficiency in our dialogues and insufficient reflection on our actions. We have not built strong collaborative relationships with our supply-chain partners to offer the consumer a compelling value proposition with unparalleled competitive advantages. The solution to our shortfall lies in the maturity of managing relationships.

CONCLUSION

The postal industry can survive the current wave of bombardment by disruptive innovation through adopting an appropriate leadership style, one based on quality relationships amongst colleagues, with suppliers, supply-chain partners and customers. The kind of leaders needed to drive this change can appreciate the personal difficulties of change and the power of looking at change from the individual point of view. Moreover, they must actively create platforms for their colleagues to apply their talents, whilst also applying consistent performance measurement and subjecting their organisation to international scrutiny. They must celebrate the gains and not shy away from acknowledging and facing the challenges.

QUESTION FOR THOUGHT AND DISCUSSION

The transformation journey explained here shows that it takes time and perseverance to drive change, with key factors being: leadership; the development of 'collective leadership' and commitment at all levels; and also strategies, tactics and approaches such as coaching. What is the relative importance of these factors and which are most crucial for driving change successfully?

Leadership in these abundant tribes or organisations looks at the world through a wide lens, giving leaders a 360-degree view of their ecosystem and helping them build a platform with a wide reach, a network of networks.

REINVENTING THE POST WITH COLLABORATIVE LEADERSHIP

Shailendra Kumar Dwivedi

India Post

INTRODUCTION

Leo Tolstoy famously observed that 'Everyone thinks of changing the world; no-one thinks of changing himself'. Does this hold true for leaders in the postal sector as they lead transformation into the 'new economy'? The need for change in posts is underlined by all stakeholders. The sector is currently reinventing itself as a three-dimensional network – with physical, electronic and financial platforms – to meet the connection and logistics needs of people with seamless flows of information, goods and money across the globe. Both the breadth and depth of the change, as well as the pace at which it needs to be implemented, accentuate the transformational challenge for postal organisations and its leaders.

There is a momentous shift taking place in the business context, from the 'Industrial Age' to the 'New Digital Age'. Do we have the kind of leadership within the postal sector that will enable it to navigate this change successfully? Has our leadership adapted its approaches, practices and behaviours sufficiently to shape the future postal network? Can our organisations move into the digital age if leadership practices and behaviours continue to draw from the 'scientific management' of the industrial age? Is the leadership in the postal sector today driving a 'new work culture' to create the 'smart post' that the world now needs? Before we can begin to answer these questions, let us look at the broader context.

THE SMART POST IN A COLLABORATIVE ECONOMY

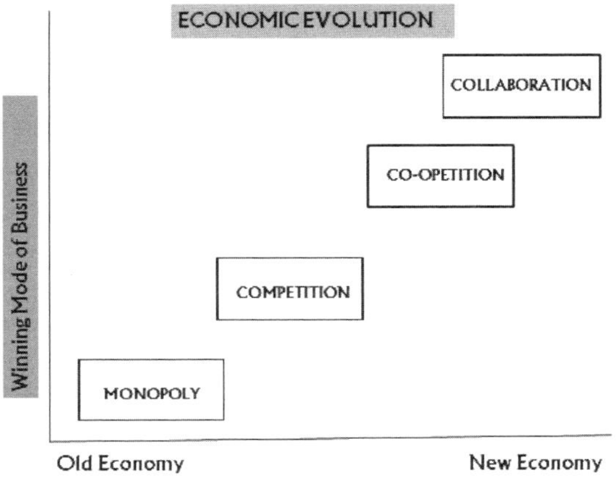

Figure 1: Economic evolution

The smart post represents a 'simple, multidimensional, agile and adaptive, resonant and trusted platform of service and technology'. The new post needs to function in an economy that is evolving as summarised in Figure 1. Successful businesses in the new economy function as a platform and a 'network of networks', facilitating collaboration for value creation, delivery and benefits to a wide group of stakeholders.

In this 'intention economy', the boundaries between suppliers, the company and customers are increasingly blurred and can function more like a circle than a linear chain. Businesses in this economy exist as an integral part of an ecosystem rather than as stand-alone fortresses. So success depends on the effective sharing of capabilities rather than hoarding; the *how* of the company is the only real advantage and not the *what*, as products and services can easily be replicated.

With the digital revolution and Web 2.0, there is an increasing transparency of information about businesses making it imperative for them to be values driven and actually 'doing the right thing'. This is evident from the importance attached to Corporate Social Responsibility (CSR) initiatives by businesses across sectors and geographies today. The external corporate reputation or brand image and the internal organisational culture are two sides of the same coin; and both are now becoming increasingly visible and important to stakeholders of the business.

With such a paradigm shift in the external context of business, can the demands on leadership remain unchanged? Do the culture and the brand of postal organisations blend well to present a consistent picture to stakeholders? Does the leadership legacy in the postal sector enable it to function as an adaptive network of networks? What leadership approaches do we need for the smart post network? Despite our long organisational history, we have more questions to explore on these fundamental points. We can find some interesting and practical answers to these questions by looking at leadership practices in successful businesses, postal and non-postal, and possibly sketch a roadmap for the leadership challenge of transforming the postal sector.

THE EVOLUTION OF LEADERSHIP AND THE REBIRTH OF THE TRIBE

With the evolution of the economy and the emergence of success stories in business such as those of Google, Zappos, Southwest Airlines, Amazon, Facebook, Salesforce. com and Intel, to name a few, the word 'maverick' has very limited application these days. Transformation stories like those of UPS and IBM and the unfolding story of postal businesses from around the world add to a rich bag of leadership tales. Are there any patterns in the development of leadership behaviour from these varied backgrounds?

In the successful businesses of today, there seems to be a departure from the age of traditional hierarchies and scientific management principles driven by the division of labour towards flatter, open structures, systems and behaviours (closer to primal human nature). Present-day successful business leadership can be viewed as harnessing our basic nature of living and working in tribes. There is, however, one important difference between aboriginal tribes and the tribes that successful businesses are working to build with globalisation and the convergence of technologies, economies, sectors and stakeholders of the 'intention economy'. The difference lies in the mindset of abundance, as opposed to that of scarcity found in the earlier tribes.

The successful business 'tribes' created by leaders across sectors are thriving on the spirit of coexistence and collaboration among tribes. This is a departure from the highly competitive, 'survival of the fittest' situation in which, in a world with scarce resources, anyone who did not belong to your tribe was considered an enemy to be beaten.

Leadership in these abundant tribes or organisations looks at the world through a wide lens, giving leaders a 360-degree view of their ecosystem and helping them build a platform with a wide reach, a network of networks, that provides hitherto unforeseen and vastly improved levels of efficiency and effectiveness by bringing together a wide range of common benefits to their stakeholders. This transition to a tribe that thrives in such an ecosystem is not easy or accidental. It requires focused and consistent leadership and organisational behaviour to progress from the current level of functioning to 'Level 5 tribal leadership'[1].

The journey for each organisation will be different depending on where they currently stand on this leadership behaviour ladder.

Leadership Level and Prevalence	Mindset	Behaviour
Level 1 (Less than 1%)	All life is bad and not worth it	These are tribes whose members are despairingly hostile – they may create scandals, steal from the company or even threaten violence
Level 2 (25%)	My life is bad, others are doing fine, I am the victim	This stage includes members who are passively antagonistic, sarcastic and resistant to new management initiatives
Level 3 (49%)	I am good, others are not	Marked by knowledge hoarders who want to out-work and out-think their competitors on an individual basis; they are lone warriors who not only want to win, but need to be the best and brightest
Level 4 (23%)	We are good, they are not	The tribe members are excited to work together for the benefit of the entire company
Level 5 (Less than 2%)	We are good, so are they	Members who have made substantial innovations seek to use their potential to make a global impact

An organisation's current level is best understood by the behaviour and beliefs of leaders and all people who belong to its 'tribe', as expressed in their language and conversations, summarised in the table above. Postal organisations, irrespective of where they are today, should naturally be programmed to thrive at Level 5 as their basic nature is to connect the world in multiple ways. In most cases currently, leadership in the posts is dealing with Level 2 and 3 behaviours and trying to take the majority to Level 4.

However, the clear goal, in the new collaborative economy, would be to take the postal sector towards Level 5. However, this cannot be achieved unless we achieve the same proficiency as organisations at Level 4 and then elevate our game to Level 5 which, arguably, is the enduring, sustainable level of leadership for posts.

---

1   *Tribal Leadership: Leveraging Natural Groups to Build a Thriving Organization* by Dave Logan, John King and Halee Fischer-Wright

Level 5 tribal leadership fits well with the individual need for self-actualisation and the collective need for transcendence beyond self-centred interests. If brought into play, it may be easier to practise and sustain than the brand of formal and stiff leadership roles and behaviours that traditional approaches tend to promote.

LEVEL 5 TRIBAL LEADERSHIP FOR POSTAL ORGANISATIONS

The need for Level 5 tribal leadership in posts is too strong to be ignored. It can be seen as the only way to position posts as the hub and enabler of a better life for the whole community each serves. The task cannot be achieved by posts alone. Being good within themselves, as within a fortress, is not enough. Posts require collaborative leadership to fulfil their mission and vision. The collaborative culture would begin from within the organisation and then embrace the wider group of stakeholders in the value circle of the entire community served by the post office. Leaders in the posts have to model the necessary behaviours on the way to this collaborative future. There are examples of such leadership within the posts today, though more as an exception than the norm.

We need to take inspiration from the positive examples to bring a fresh approach to postal leadership. Collaborative leadership thrives on a shared vision, open communication, flatter structures, effective knowledge management, team learning, systems and design thinking. The leaders have to design and shape the organisational architecture (structure, systems and behaviours) in a way that supports the growth of the individuals in the tribe to ensure they are happy themselves and are ready to deliver happiness to the larger community, with the post office as the pivotal platform or network of networks.

The basic individual needs of autonomy, significance, self-mastery, learning and growth can be fulfilled by leaders who are committed to creating a workplace that provides the necessary space and opportunities while creating and delivering the desired value to its customers and other stakeholders. An organisational culture that is guided by a meta-goal of sustainability and community development and values of professionalism, egalitarianism, philanthropy, individuality, respect and integrity can fuel the passion of postal employees.

This frame, much wider than the traditional products and services of the posts, can help leaders provide a sense of purpose for their teams and make their efforts and contribution more meaningful for every individual involved in the postal endeavour with their communities. Postal organisations are not naturally designed to play the game of competition. They excel when they have a larger benefit to deliver to their customers. This used to be the traditional universal service obligation but the new economy needs a synergistic logistics platform from the postal operators to bring a better life in a more sustainable and modern way by enabling the efficient exchange of goods, money and information through the postal network. This role can be fulfilled by the posts only if their leaders and employees at all levels are able to model Level 5 tribal leadership behaviours.

CONCLUSION

In the present business context, posts require a bold new approach to leadership that is in line with their business goals and roles. Level 5 tribal leadership is a good reference point for collaborative leadership. We can draw a roadmap for leadership in the posts on this basic premise.

The onus is on leaders to begin the change within themselves; then, in order to lead in the collaborative economy, we need greater collaborative leadership. The manifesto for leadership for posts is clear if we believe in our collaborative future. To what Leo Tolstoy famously said, Mahatma Gandhi had a famous and successful practice that can be a guiding principle for all leaders at all times. Mahatma Gandhi's practice can be summarised with the words: 'Be the change you want to see in the world.'

QUESTION FOR THOUGHT AND DISCUSSION

What issues and challenges currently faced by postal companies and industry associations would be resolved by a more collaborative, Level 5 tribal style of leadership? What would be the implications of this and what kind of cooperation and collaboration could be envisaged across the whole sector?

...creating a network and a platform for sharing different kinds of experiences and excellent practice of doing good but that is also good business – in other words, financially positive, socially right and environmentally friendly.

IN SUSTAINABILITY, NO BUSINESS IS AN ISLAND

Liene Norberg and Derek Osborn

SCALE Advantage

INTRODUCTION

When people talk about 'sustainability' in the postal sector, they usually touch upon the reduction of CO_2 emissions or maybe the reduction of waste or energy consumption. Moreover, the understanding of sustainability has often been 'locked' into the corporate social responsibility frame or, in some cases, has never left the managerial-level discussion of delivering sustainable quarterly growth of volumes. In other words, the word is widely used but with very many different meanings.

Despite the most recent trend in which sustainability has become a fashionable talking point, beyond environmentalists, sometimes even hitting the top of big-business agendas (mostly for better brand appearance or corporate reputation), it is still mainly considered a 'nice to do' option rather than a 'must do'.

LEADING WITH SUCCESS *AND* SUCCESSION IN FOCUS

In this century in which everyone has heard about the global climate change, increasing human population on earth, depleting natural resources and businesses blindly striving for the kind of growth this planet may not be able to support, business leaders need to step outside these current frames and view the challenges more broadly and address them strategically. At the same time, a new generation of business leaders and consumers is about to enter the market, with sustainability deeply rooted into their personal beliefs and values.

The fact that businesses need to change their approach and innovate towards broader and longer-term sustainability is obvious. If we continue to address these social, economic and environmental aspects merely from the problem-solving angle and wait for someone else (governments, NGOs or consumers) to lead the change, we may never experience the turning point – or it may come too late.

Sustainability in its widest sense is about systems – supply chains, human resources, operations etc. – and how they communicate and interact with each other. Most importantly, considering what impact they have on business in the long run, these include communities, customers and the environment around them. As a result, sustainability has an effect on practically everything, delivering outcomes in many strategically important areas such as efficiency, change management, people motivation and involvement, innovation, long-term decision making, brand value, market access and meeting customer demands, to name just a few.

We have been pleased to see several really good examples of companies and organisations within the postal sector taking the lead in responding to these global challenges. They are different from others because they have chosen to view sustainability strategically, through a prism of long-term value creation that goes beyond temporary gains while eliminating short-termism from their business decision-making practices. In other words, they are beginning to set a completely new benchmark for Corporate Sustainability Leadership within the postal industry.

To find out more about how the postal industry is responding to the sustainability challenge, we gathered these 'sustainability ambassadors' together for a workshop. In doing so, we were creating a network and a platform for sharing different kinds of experiences and excellent practices of doing good but that is also good business – in other words, financially positive, socially right and environmentally friendly.

A WORKSHOP PLATFORM FOR MULTIPLYING THE VALUE OF SHARED EXPERIENCES

When forming the participant base for this first meeting, we had a principle in focus that could be best described by rephrasing the famous quote of John Donne: in sustainability, *no business is an island.*

Besides the leading postal companies we also invited the main industry suppliers and member organisations. Being a part of the same value chain, each of them acknowledged their interdependencies and the positive impact of collaborative effort where everyone is collectively involved and accountable.

An important outcome from this newly founded network is that we got to hear many inspiring stories from companies in different positions but all in the same sector, companies of different sizes and levels of sustainability development and integration. Some of them have developed strong business cases for sustainability, both in efficiency and new revenue streams; some have innovated, moving their business models towards sustainability; whilst others are focused on building awareness and need more examples of good practice. However, and of equally importance, we heard about ideas that people had tried and that didn't work – but lessons were learnt and shared. In this group, we view failure as an integral part of innovation. We are also keen on making new links with companies in other sectors, to see what transferable learning is possible with the addition of different perspectives and approaches. There are many opportunities for coaching and mentoring each other whilst also expanding the network to reach deeper into the postal value chain.

Being a part of the same value chain, different stakeholders have a unique possibility to achieve a synergy of outcomes together through a collective approach. We saw some exciting examples both from the posts and industry suppliers. The latter demonstrate the ability to deliver solutions according to customers' needs while demonstrating care for the environment and the communities they operate in.

For example, Vanderlande Industries has made a commitment to cradle-to-cradle design when creating equipment for postal operations, and Neopost's innovation responds to the core need of their postal consumers for efficiency, whilst also minimising the environmental footprint along the whole postal supply chain. Further down the line, the post also listens to its customers carefully and demonstrates equally strong leadership in delivering their items, whilst thinking about their people, the society they operate in and the environmental impact. With all these stakeholders collaborating, the postal industry can make a positive and stronger collective contribution to the future sustainability of the industry and the planet.

Other examples include La Poste which took a strategic leadership role in a consortium to commission the supply of electric vehicles for its home market and is the founder of the Postal Carbon Fund which is financing projects in developing countries. More and more companies are moving towards a 'circular economy' and some have even developed so far that they make business with their experience. DPD is developing the total-zero mind-set at no cost to their customers and CTT Correios have developed a range of 'sustainable' products and services.

All these examples demonstrate the value of strong leadership in this area and these companies can in no way be described as compliance focused. They have made brave decisions to integrate sustainability into their business strategy, operating models and organisation. In other words, they address sustainability as a key business imperative.

BENCHMARKING SURVEY

For the workshop, we carried out an initial benchmarking study that would take a snapshot of the industry as it stands today. First, we looked at how sustainability is defined inside these companies. The results showed that sustainability integration in the post is more focused on the social aspect, with the environmental aspect becoming increasingly important – which is not surprising for a labour-intensive business. Among these leaders, however, 65% of the surveyed companies responded that within their organisations sustainability is viewed as a complex issue including social, environmental and economic aspects.

Through the study we discovered that some of these companies have integrated sustainability in their mission statements and some even in their company visions. When it comes to corporate strategy among the postal companies, the strategic focus lies on social and economic sustainability, while the main industry suppliers naturally look towards environment and efficiency that helps their customers to gain competitive advantage while saving costs, material and energy.

Importantly nearly all the companies in the survey had linked their corporate goals to sustainability, which demonstrates that they really take sustainability seriously and that it is inextricably linked to their performance and their future.

When we asked these companies if they think that they are considered successful in sustainability by their main stakeholders, the majority replied that they can always improve. The most important areas for improvement were identified as: communication to key stakeholder groups, integrating sustainability in the core business, investing in sustainable technology and supporting innovation; and some expressed a need to become more transparent. The latter is of great importance because transparency is a basis for trust.

'We need to be clear about what we do and why we do it', they said. More importantly, trust should work both ways, across the whole value chain. This is also linked to customer behaviour, as it was readily acknowledged that customers often do not base their purchasing decisions on sustainability factors. However, it is becoming common to rate companies according to their sustainability performance, and it is likely that this trend will increasingly impact on the postal sector.

We also asked about the CEO's attitude towards sustainability and in 60% of cases postal-sector CEOs consider sustainability as being 'strategically important'. Furthermore, 25% of CEOs in our survey think that sustainability is 'who we are', meaning that it is mirrored in the companies raison d'être and rooted in its values and the values of its employees. All CEOs agreed that sustainability is not a regulatory issue but, at the same time, in 15% of companies it was not on the top of the agenda for their executives yet.

IMPLEMENTING CHANGE

These companies, the 'postal industry sustainability leaders', value sustainable customer relationships rather than quick gains and they continuously seek new ways to innovate and engage their people in this journey. It was said by one participant that: 'Everything we do, we do with our people. Everything we do, we do on this planet'.

For change to be effective, it needs to reach all levels of an organisation. Through the study we discovered that, in the postal business, responsibility for sustainability is either with the middle (35%) or top (35%) management levels, with sustainability being integrated in the regional structures in only 15% of cases and having the support of the highest organisation level (board) in only 15% of cases. This shows that there is much work to be done in establishing sustainability as part of institutional leadership structures within organisations and that there is a need to promote active leadership (or educating leaders) to drive systematic change.

The positive news was that, in the companies in which sustainability is represented at middle management level (Sustainability Department) to top management level, it is expected to increase in importance. Typically in the postal sector, this is a one- or few-person department, which is organisationally isolated, with great pressure from the stakeholders and no real authority. These sustainability leaders need to reach certain people in the organisation who have more authority in order to get things done. Moreover, we learned that in those companies without clear top-level support, no changes are expected within the next five years. This highlights a clear leadership challenge, especially as the sustainability champions acknowledged that no real change is possible without clear top-level commitment driving it. This is a crucial precondition, taking into account a study by the Network For Business Sustainability which asserts that even 'personal beliefs do not affect sustainable behaviour – people really take their tone from the top'.[1]

---

1   Network for Business Sustainability

One of the most difficult questions that we also addressed was how to get everyone involved. This was clearly visualised and articulated by the success story of bpost's transformational change. Ideas from their leadership engagement with people for change included these comments: *They will be positive about it (change) if they feel that there is commitment from the top and if there is trust. The more connected they feel, the closer they get to associating themselves with the new company culture of sustainability. Leaders who have been able to turn around underperforming companies focus on succession and visible leadership. They speak with all the employees and don't just produce strategies and distribute plans. Taking people with you and making sure they share your vision and help you develop it is critical. So then they can carry the torch after the leader is gone or not present. Spreading leadership is done by making it a shared responsibility.*

The results of the study also showed that today 'the average employee' in the postal sector thinks that sustainability is important, but that it is not the priority issue. Even more worrying was the fact that 17% think that sustainability is not important at all to their employees. However, in 8% of cases there is a chance that people would care more if they were paid for their 'sustainability' performance.

From the study we also understood the current situation of the sustainability leaders regarding their position and leverage. In most of the companies, it was felt that sustainability leaders should be granted more authority than they have today and that they would also prefer sustainability to be viewed more broadly, covering not just a single aspect (e.g. environmental): instead, their scope of influence should stretch across social, economic and environmental aspects of sustainability. The role of the sustainability leader at this point becomes even more challenging – they need to convince not only their peers and leaders, but also all stakeholders and shareholders of the benefits of sustainability.

MAKING SUSTAINABILITY 'SELLABLE'

The experts acknowledged that it is still very difficult to 'sell' sustainability within a business. This is mostly because it is difficult to find a convincing business case for it in terms of revenue generation or return on investment in the conventional sense, and because the customer is not yet ready to pay extra for it. Sustainability should be for free, they pointed out, because if we want something to be truly sustainable, we can't make it a luxury that is optional and has to be paid extra for.

There are a few companies that see sustainability from the prism of efficiency gains and saving money, but most of them still find it difficult to sell not only to the customer, but even to their colleagues, other departments and especially the shareholder.

The advice from the sustainability ambassadors was that, at this stage, sustainability should be viewed through efficiency gains and calculated in real money. Moreover, the best examples should be highlighted even more than they are. The principle of 'if they can do it, we can do it' works well across the postal value chain. Besides that, we all should become better at storytelling as we are surrounded by many great examples within the industry.

There are also visible examples outside the industry and companies with big names have proved that the link can and does exist between sustainability and financial performance. In other words, there is no need to compromise between people, planet and performance and where the value gained from the company's operations is shared between the various stakeholders. Research has shown that companies who are doing well are also usually doing good and have been able to build a successful business case around sustainability.[2]

The effect of sustainability is becoming more symbolically visible as we see global corporations making use of green in their logos – these include McDonald's, which is painting its red logo background green; Coca Cola, whose bottle has grown green leaves; and even Apple, whose apple logo has also received a green leaf. Companies are building brand value, reputation and enhancing other intangible assets through sustainability and showing that they care. Moreover, they are being rated according to their sustainability performance by investors and customers who measure their social and environmental impacts throughout the supply chain. But sustainability has to be more than 'green-washing' as the world is becoming more and more transparent, especially with the prevalence of social media.

Our study results showed that a great majority of respondents would expect stronger leadership from the general consumer in making the 'right' choice and demanding more good sustainable services and products. Nearly 30% think that leadership on sustainability should come from national governments in setting more ambitious targets, supported by innovations; while 20% of the companies believe that stronger leadership should come from the business world. Moreover, within the business world there is an agreement that it should be a collaborative

---

2   Michael Beer, Russell A. Eisenstat, Nathaniel Foote, Tobias Fredberg and Flemming Norrgren, Higher Ambition: How Great Leaders *Create Economic and Social Value*, Harvard Business Press Books, 2011

effort where every little initiative and achievement towards a more sustainable future is appraised and valued.

CONCLUSION

Sustainable business is about goals that matter and goes beyond temporary gains, focusing on value creation at all levels. A leader who really takes sustainability seriously, accepts responsibility for wider social, economic and environmental areas that are affected by his or her influence. It is a fact that every company has to do good business. But the benefits to the customer from being more sustainable also need to be clearly articulated.

Business leaders of today should leave the task of delivering positive financial results to managers and focus instead on building a long-lasting legacy, learning to navigate these complex socio-economic-environmental systems and manage increasingly important stakeholder relations. Broad cross-sector leadership may be one of the replies to this challenge because in the end every enterprise is bound up with every other – no business is an island. If there are business leaders who still do not see the point in this, they should ask themselves this simple question: what do you want to be remembered for?

QUESTION FOR THOUGHT AND DISCUSSION

What are the opportunities for real cross-sector strategic leadership on sustainability issues and what are some of the steps that can help make this possible? What can the postal sector learn about sustainability leadership from manufacturing, retail, supply-chain logistics – or indeed any other sector?

SECTION 3
CHANGING THE WAY POSTS OPERATE

Edited by Jacob Johnsen

Ipostes

From the outside, it could seem that nothing much has changed in postal operations over time. Customers still see that they hand over their postal items to the post and that these are delivered in a quick, trustworthy, secure and well-managed manner. Little do they know that some major changes are taking place within postal operations.

The following section outlines, from four different perspectives, how operational practices continue to be challenged by new requirements, market changes and endless technological possibilities.

Amine Khechfé analyses the main postal challenges of international e-commerce delivery and identifies solutions for returns as well as speedy same-day delivery as the two main areas of improvements. For a smooth return solution, posts must fully integrate their systems and the author concludes that the postal operator is ideally suited when it comes to same-day delivery, given its local presence and strong infrastructure.

Alain Roset makes the point that the good old letterbox is challenged by the evolution of the market and the exchanges between the economic actors over the last 10 years: the digital networks take a larger part of the exchange of information formerly transmitted by letters and the exchanges of goods increase rapidly. The letterbox must move to becoming a parcel box or disappear altogether.

Adrian King looks at how the development and adoption of mobile systems can help postal companies meet their business challenges over the next five years. Whilst many posts are now on their third implementation of a mobile infrastructure, the potential operational and customer benefits inherent in having a 'near real-time distributed computing infrastructure' connecting customers, receivers, operational centres and delivery workers have not yet been exploited.

Michael Faltum shows how an ever-changing, developing and challenging technological landscape can be managed so that the operator can identify the 'low-hanging fruits', combine new technological possibilities and stay abreast of technological evolution.

Postal organisations must be willing to innovate and adapt to the new technological landscape in order to keep up. By embracing delivery options like international returns and same-day shipping, the postal industry can not only compete, but also thrive.

WHERE THE POSTAL INDUSTRY IS HEADING NEXT: GLOBAL MARKET AND SAME-DAY SHIPPING

Amine Khechfé

Endicia

INTRODUCTION

When you think of the postal industry, the words 'cutting-edge' and 'innovation' may not come to mind. The postal industry typically is associated with conservative positioning and a sluggish adoption of new technologies.

But that way of thinking no longer holds true. The postal industry is undergoing a transformation – and technology is the game-changer. Technological advances have opened-up many interesting areas of emerging growth in the postal industry: two of these are global returns and same-day shipping.

Global returns come into play when considering the huge growth in cross-border e-commerce. In fact, according to research by Triangle Management Services, revenues generated by online retailers selling internationally are predicted to almost triple by 2015[1]. It makes sense then that postal organisations are jumping on this global market trend. However, cross-border e-commerce can get a little sticky, especially when it comes to returns. A complicated returns process can be a major

---

1   Source: http://postandparcel.info/51406/news/markets/visibility-reliability-key-to-success-in-booming-cross-border-ecommerce

deal-breaker for online shoppers, especially if they are purchasing from another country. It is essential that companies refine their international returns policies and procedures with the consumer in mind and that the postal organisations expand their products and services to meet that need.

Another hot topic in the postal world, driven by consumer interest, is same-day delivery. In today's world, e-commerce businesses are constantly struggling to keep up with consumers' increasing desire for instant gratification. So when same-day shipping came on the scene, private carriers, regional carriers, local couriers and e-commerce giants like Amazon, eBay and Google jumped in, determined to deliver faster and cheaper than the rest of the competition. Same-day shipping currently is available only in a few select cities, but at the current pace it will not be long before it becomes the norm in e-commerce delivery.

As these e-commerce trends develop, postal operators around the world are reacting and in some cases leading the innovation. Contrary to popular belief, the postal industry is far from dying. E-commerce is spurring new growth and opportunity for the posts, driving an average parcel volume increase of 5.8% from 2011 to 2012, according to Accenture[2]. USPS alone saw parcel volume growth of 6% from FY2012 to FY2013[3]. But postal organisations must be willing to innovate and adapt to the new technological landscape in order to keep up. By embracing delivery options like international returns and same-day shipping, the postal industry can not only compete, but also thrive.

GLOBAL RETURNS

Research shows that returning a package is a huge pain point for online shoppers and sellers alike. A ComScore study (2012) revealed that 42% of e-commerce consumers seek a simple return and exchange process – the second-highest-cited desire, right behind free and discounted shipping. Not surprisingly, in another ComScore study (2013), 85% of customers said they will not give repeat business if the return process is inconvenient. Moreover, 95% of online consumers say they will shop again at businesses offering a convenient returns experience. In fact, in that same study, if an online retailer offers a hassle-free returns policy, 67%

---

2   Source: Achieving High Performance in the Postal Industry, Accenture Research and Insights 2014, Accenture, 2014

3   Source: Despite Revenue Growth and Record Productivity, Postal Service Loses $5 Billion in 2013 Fiscal Year, available from: http://about.usps.com/news/national-releases/2013/pr13_087.htm (accessed November 2013)

of respondents would shop more with that retailer and an impressive 64% would recommend the retailer to a friend.

If an online retailer offers a hassle-free returns policy, I will...

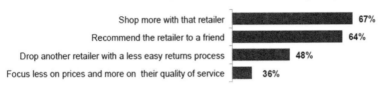

Figure 1: Impact of returns process on shopper experience

The desire for a smooth returns experience does not vary when consumers purchase from a country other than their own. Yet this is a difficult proposition: it is expensive via private carriers and not always possible via postal operators. According to the 2014 Copenhagen Economics Delivery Operator Questionnaire, cross-border returns are generally not as available via postal operators as domestic returns. The Copenhagen Economics research showed that only 15% of national postal operators in Europe allow cross-border e-shoppers to return parcels by handing them in at a local post office or collection point. If posts could share a common platform to ease cross-border shipments and returns, they would increase their competitive standing as it relates to gaining increased e-commerce business.

No doubt, the competition in the returns space is fierce. A glimpse into the competitive landscape reveals private carriers, like UPS and FedEx, at the top of the value chain, in many cases because they allow 'pay-on-use' returns shipping labels (i.e. the shipper does not pay for the cost of the shipping until the shipment has actually entered the mail stream). These international parcel carriers deliver high-quality value propositions – each as a cohesive single brand on a global scale – that threaten postal operators' business.

Other postal competitors include e-commerce marketplace and platform providers such as eBay, Amazon and Google Shopping. These businesses offer a wide array of fulfilment and delivery services, ranging from warehousing and fulfilment for themselves and their sellers (Amazon has 108 active fulfilment centres around the world as of May 2014, with 19 more slated to open), as well as pick-up points and lockers on the delivery side. Increasingly, postal operators are seeing competition in the last mile, with companies sure to emulate Amazon's April 2014 announcement that it will start operating its own trucks for the last-mile delivery of Amazon products.

So how can postal operators compete? Through optimised technology and strategic partnerships. As a trusted partner of the USPS and other postal operators, Endicia is developing an omni-channel shipping technology platform that serves as a common platform for postal operators around the world, enabling innovations such as domestic and cross-border returns through a single integrated platform.

In 2014, Endicia launched a pay-on-use returns program in the US. Through this program, postage is paid only if and when the return label is used. The customers report an improved and hassle-free returns experience for their consumers. Additionally, customers save considerable time since the technology eliminates the need to monitor and request refunds for pre-paid labels that are never used. Most importantly, by not pre-paying for labels, customers eliminate the risk of losing money on unused postage labels.

Figure 2: Pay-on-use return label

Creating partnerships with and between postal operators around the world is a critical success factor for overcoming competitive pressures. Currently, private carriers like UPS and FedEx are positioned as single vendors around the world. There is an opportunity for posts also to offer one seamless international shipping experience. For example, Endicia already has a relationship with Canada Post to return parcels to the US. Domestic sellers can purchase and create Canada Post shipping labels. The sellers can then email (or send) the label to the consumer in Canada who wants to make a return; the consumer then simply needs to put the label on the package and drop it off at any Canada Post retail location. Canada Post brings the package into the US and it is delivered by the US Postal service. Domestic sellers are billed in US$.

Through our partnership with the Canada Post, sellers can benefit from rates and services that make the cost of returns from Canada cheaper than the original export shipment from the US. We should add that the reverse is also true: a Canadian merchant with customers in the US can also leverage Endicia's technologies to allow for that seamless postal channel experience to return products back to Canada. By providing labelling solutions on both sides of the border and handling the currency exchange, the platform is able to accomplish something that is very difficult for postal authorities to do today: to act as one network in reverse logistics. As we expand this returns solution to new postal markets, it will only enhance postal networks and bring more competition to commercial carriers such as FedEx and UPS.

EMERGING GROWTH: THE SAME-DAY DELIVERY MARKET

Same-day delivery has recently emerged as an important development towards making e-commerce *the* premiere choice for everyday shopping. As a result, everyone – from e-commerce tech companies to tried-and-true postal couriers – is experimenting with ways to get product delivered to the consumer in the shortest amount of time possible.

Today, same-day shipping has only been available in select cities through programs such as Amazon, Google Shopping Express, eBay Now and the USPS's Metro Post. However, it will not be long before same-day delivery becomes available everywhere, and when that happens, the US Postal Service is in a prime position to own the market.

The USPS has three distinct advantages when it comes to same-day shipping. First, they have a fleet of delivery vehicles readily available to make residential shipments, meaning they would not need to invest in additional infrastructure. Second, they have a troop of postal couriers who are familiar with the nuances and challenges of certain residential delivery routes, such as apartment complexes and gated communities. And third, the USPS is vendor and recipient-neutral: they are not tied to any one commercial company and are able therefore to offer same-day shipping services to anyone.

If we look at the global sector, the United States is slightly behind the game when it comes to same-day shipping. Many foreign carriers, such as Posten AB in Sweden and bpost in Belgium, have found success by offering a same-day grocery service. While the USPS is not equipped to handle grocery delivery at this time (as it would require refrigerated trucks), this is another area of possible expansion for them.

Ultimately, the key to same-day shipping success lies in having an adjustable delivery network (i.e. dynamic routing) that would allow couriers continually to identify the most direct service route at a given point in time – for example, the route taken might be different at 10:30am from that at 5pm. Merchants looking to offer same-day delivery also face the challenge of educating their customers about the service. While same-day shipping has yet to reach the consumer expectation and availability of free shipping, one thing's for sure: it will be an important element in the future of e-commerce delivery.

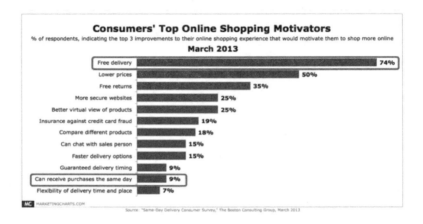

Figure 3: Results of consumer survey on top online shopping motivators

CONCLUSION

As consumers demand simplified returns policies and experiences, and as both companies and consumers explore same-day services, the posts are well positioned to compete. E-commerce will continue to fuel innovation at a rapid pace and the posts will need to identify those key technologies with the biggest – and quickest – impact, paired with the strategic partnerships that can help them deliver and lead.

QUESTION FOR THOUGHT AND DISCUSSION

A suitable and simple returns process is required for the global postal marketplace. How can postal operators include customs in such a process and ease the return of paid duties in the case of returns? How can one envisage a common global system for international returns with individual postal operators that have optimised their systems mainly for national mail, and are guided by national regulatory bodies?

The old letterbox receiving two or three thin letters per day will in the future receive and secure parcels that are bigger and bigger, but only arrive on fewer days per year.

THE LETTERBOXES OF THE FUTURE

Alain Roset

La Poste

INTRODUCTION

The origin of a device able to receive physical messages lies in the middle of the fourteenth century, with the first 'tamburi' around the Doge's Palace in Venice. This was mainly intended to provide anonymity to the sender and in fact the usual letterbox came later. The letterbox is part of the history of postal operators: collection boxes have existed since the sixteenth century and individual letterboxes since the nineteenth. This latter century was when mail began its expansion, after the invention of the stamp.

Since this time, the functionalities of the letterbox have remained identical around the world. In Europe, a CEN standard fixes:

- The size of the slot for an easy introduction of the letters. The slot is a physical equivalent of the 'one-way' algorithms used to encrypt messages, making it easy to introduce letters whilst their collection is reserved to the person with the key.

- The levels of physical security for the content.

This old companion of our homes and the work tool of millions of mail carriers around the world is now challenged. The source for this is the evolution of the market for different exchanges between economic actors over a decade: the digital networks now take a larger part of the exchange of information formerly transmitted by letters. Meanwhile, the exchange of goods increases rapidly. The letterbox must become a parcel box or disappear altogether.

FROM THE LETTERBOX TO THE PARCEL BOX: A 'NOT SO EASY' TRANSFORMATION

The old letterbox receiving two or three thin letters per day will in the future receive and secure parcels that are bigger and bigger, but only arrive on fewer days per year.

The new functionalities are easy to define:

- A size large enough to receive most of the parcels – this functionality supercedes the 'one way' of the slot

- A security level that is high enough to secure the goods before collection by the receiver, and with more requirements than needed for the security of the mail

- An authentication tool to prove the exchange between the logistic operator and the receiver

- A low cost in order to have a rapid deployment.

Actually, providers have found solutions for two user cases:

1. The parcel box owned by the logistics operator, shared between many receivers so as rapidly to reach the threshold of efficiency, and

2. The parcel box owned by the receiver for his/her own use, who bears all the costs of a relatively sparse use.

These first solutions proposed by operators and suppliers are based on groups of tens of boxes installed outside, 'around the corner' or in the lobby of buildings, in a place easy to access for the receiver. These solutions are well-suited for sparse receivers of parcels, reduce the cost of the 'last mile' and the cost of the absence of the receiver, and finally reduce the transaction costs.

The change of all the letterboxes in Europe represents a cost of around €25 billion, with the potential of reducing this to €2–3 billion by sharing between receivers and the logistics operators.

To help the rapid deployment of the parcel boxes, a European standard is being adopted to fix the different sizes (including eight capacity levels to try to influence the e-merchants market to pack the goods in the most suitable packages) and also the different levels of security.

THE PARCEL BOX AND A PARALLEL APPROACH WITH TELECOM NETWORKS

If we compare the evolution since the '60s of the terminals of the telecom networks with the terminals of the postal networks, we note a large difference. Telecom terminals have increased their features drastically, from simple analogue phones in the '60s, through digital phones with features in the '80s (memory of phone numbers, then message memory, etc.), then mobiles phone terminals in the '90s, then boxes able to provide phone, data exchanges and now video services.

An analysis of the evolution of the telecom network enables the design of some trends for the postal terminals, while paying attention to the similarities and differences. The main characteristics of the telecom market may prove useful to understand the parcel-box evolutions:

Characteristics of the telecom market	Questions requiring solution for the parcel box market
The success of the explosion of the telecom terminals is a subtle mix of standards to guarantee interoperability and competition to stimulate the innovation of the market.	How to repeat the success of the telecom market in the market for parcel delivery? By standardisation for interoperability and competition.
The terminals are independent of the network but for economic reasons the operator may limit the connection of the terminal to its own network, covering the cost of the terminal.	Where several e-merchants will merge their flows of parcels to use the same parcel boxes: in front of the equipment or upstream, can the terminal remain under the control of a single operator?
	Is the standardisation at European level of the sizes and the levels of security of the parcel boxes enough? Is it possible to add more standardised interfaces at national levels?
The basic telecom networks have generated the birth of added-value services ('over the top') like social networks and digital TV service providers with a strong struggle between the different layers to share the worldwide revenues. The largest margin is now more for the added-service providers than for basic telecom services.	How to share the benefit between all the stakeholders of the value chain – from the owner of the parcel boxes up to the provider of goods for the marketplaces of the e-merchants?

Characteristics of the telecom market	Questions requiring solution for the parcel box market
Revenues were originally connected directly to use, then 'all-inclusive' prices emerged and, finally, the introduction of value-added services 'over the top' have put in place new pricing methods like the inclusion of advertisements in the messages or the capture and selling of information towards the end user.	Who will secure the investment to renew the multitude of letterboxes? Is it possible to invest only with the scope of the efficiency of the 'last mile'? Are other business models viable, other than the pay per use adapted to this device?
The IP protocol is the keystone of the telecom exchanges.	What new exchange protocol will emerge to manage the flows of data linked with physical items?

THE PARCEL BOX – A TERMINAL OF THE INTERNET OF THINGS

A new start-up was present at the Consumer Electronics Show in Las Vegas in January 2014. The company Signée presented a concept of parcel box 'click and connect at home' as a first element of the 'Internet of things'. It is able to exchange data with different stakeholders in the 'last-mile' delivery, with the e-merchant, with the receiver through the web and, in the future, directly with the parcel itself, if electronic tags are included in the label.

This view of the parcel box in the middle of a '3.0 network' is quite new and opens up the possibility of using parcel boxes as a universal hub for the exchange of physical goods. In this future, the management of data is fundamental, as part of a close relationship with the receiver – the centre of the business for all different levels of the value chain from the e-merchant to the logistics provider.

The old letterbox will catch up with telecom equipment centred only on the exchange of data, by playing a strategic role in the exchange of the goods.

CONCLUSION

The parcel delivery market is moving rapidly, with many innovations from incumbent operators and many start-ups showing that the market of e-commerce is not yet fully stratified. There are many possible ways to develop more delivery functionalities for the satisfaction of the receivers, guided by ideas from the telecom market.

ANNEX: future standardised sizes of the parcel boxes

SIZE of the PARCELBOX	PARCELS DIMENSIONS in mm			VOLUME in litres
XXS	200	140	80	2,2
XS	200	300	80	4,8
S	210	330	120	8,3
M	230	330	260	19,7
L	230	330	500	38
XL	340	400	530	72
XXL	400	500	700	140
XXXL	400	600	1000	240

QUESTION FOR THOUGHT AND DISCUSSION

There is a clear need to modernise the letterbox – will this evolution require that all service providers collaborate to develop future post or parcel boxes? How then should the costs and benefits be shared between all the stakeholders of the value chain: from the owner of the parcel boxes up to the provider of goods for the marketplaces of the e-merchants? Do postal operators have an advantageous position and an opportunity to play a leading role in these developments?

The visibility and distribution of information through mobile networks and devices between receivers, merchants' systems and carrier operations' systems will be a fundamental component of building agile productive companies.

DRIVING PRODUCTIVITY THROUGH MOBILITY

Adrian King
Strategia Group

INTRODUCTION

How can the development and adoption of mobile systems help postal companies meet current and future business challenges?

Many posts have implemented a mobile infrastructure; however, the potential operational and customer benefits inherent in having a 'near-real-time distributed computing infrastructure' for connecting customers, receivers, operational centres and delivery workers often have not yet been explored or exploited. Indeed, it could be argued that posts need to develop and commit to a mobile vision, which embraces these kinds, or opportunities that are created by an ever-expanding network of 'persistently connected' mobile eco-systems of receivers, merchants and employees.

The aim has to be deliberately wide-ranging and high-level as it seeks to stimulate imagination about possibility rather than define solutions, business cases and implementation plans.

BUSINESS CHALLENGE

Most posts face a number of significant business challenges:

- Productivity has been greatly increased through automation. However, because of the success of these programmes, the marginal additional benefits to be gained through this route are diminishing and additional areas of productivity innovation have to be found and exploited.

- A key factor in building future productivity will be the ability to create intelligent and agile operational systems where work is more closely aligned to volumes and unnecessary processes are reduced. Information flows and labour utilisation will be critical to the success of this approach.

- The composition of the business is shifting, with packets and parcels becoming increasingly important revenue streams.

- The market dynamics and delivery economics of packets and parcels are different and more competitive. There is a greater need for customer interaction and increased need for receiver-driven delivery preferences as well as pressure to drive up first-time hit rates to improve merchant/receiver loyalty and minimise operational costs.

- The management and exploitation of integrated information along with physical delivery will become a significant part of both the operational process and the customer value proposition.

Consequently, the ability of a mobile infrastructure to support resource alignment and agility is one of the essential tools which can support both the enhancement of operational efficiency and a greatly improved customer value proposition.

MOBILE INFRASTRUCTURES

It is a reasonably safe planning assumption that mobile infrastructures will continue to develop in ways that increase the potential richness of the platform – for example, the introduction of features to enable increased network coverage, at falling costs and with higher data speeds, at the same time providing more functional rugged handsets. Together with improvements in mobile enterprise application platform strategies (MEAPS) and application programming interfaces (APIs) and comparable solutions, such developments will enable more flexible upgrading and investment cycles and so enhance the ability to integrate best-of-breed applications and reduce development and maintenance costs. In combination with an 'app-based' receiver culture and a more naturally 'mobile-literate' workforce, this makes it an obvious platform to exploit in the future.

There is a wide variance in the use of mobile platforms between geographies and countries; however, developments can be grouped into three main categories: visibility, carrier/driver management and customer interaction. The next section discusses core and developmental trends in each area.

VISIBILITY, PROOF OF DELIVERY (POD) AND BAR CODES

To date, the dominant area for the use of mobile is in the creation of pipeline visibility. The goal has been to generate productivity benefit through process and operational changes.

CORE APPLICATIONS

- Rationalisation of back-office functions through the enhanced loading and reconciliation of dispatch manifests

- Reduction in loading times enabling quicker turnarounds and greater hours on the road

- Enhanced fleet utilisation through dispatch managers working with drivers on dynamic collections and adjusting to traffic conditions

- Collection of POD scan events uploaded in near real time to own and/or merchant websites to reduce utilisation of customer-service call centres – the trend would appear to be moving from reporting exception events to giving the receiver access to visibility along the whole pipeline as a response to a new generation of receivers who want 'a relationship to their parcel' from the point of purchase.

Emerging applications include:

- The growing use of 'proof of presence' scans which creates a lower cost engagement with the customer and has been proven to improve collection and default rates on local taxation letter demands

- Use of encrypted bar codes on letter items which enable senders to put client confidential information on to the letter to improve the efficiency of integrated business processes

- Use of photographs by the delivery company either to document damaged items or to create a record of 'safe place' drops.

Visibility to enable agile resource allocation will continue to be a key goal of a mobility-driven productivity agenda.

DRIVER AND CARRIER MANAGEMENT

Raising delivery productivity for both multiple packet/letter carriers and parcel drivers is arguably one of the most significant challenges for the industry so, not surprisingly, there is thus considerable interest in using mobile infrastructures to meet this goal.

There are two main areas of focus for interaction. Firstly, the migration of cab-based systems to the mobile environment and secondly, driver support and driver management. One major postal integrator described this as the 'next opportunity for using mobile to transform the business'.

CORE APPLICATIONS

- The goal is to move all functions related to vehicle, driver management and productivity from cab-based technology onto the handheld device. The benefits are seen as reduced capital cost, reduced application-management costs and flexibility if the vehicles are off the road.

- This is being further extended to integrate cab and driver alarms into mobile, and also to use the core mobile device and intelligent packaging to measure temperature conditions and range for sensitive goods.

Emerging applications include:

- System prompts to ensure delivery process compliance

- GPS to track and monitor vehicles' actual routes and match to optimised route

- Measurement of driver time utilisation

- Use for clock-in/clock-out if driver/worker is not depot based

- Eco-driving fuel utilisation

- Legal driving compliance.

A related area of interest is the use of mobile technology to support letter carrier rounds. The carrier downloads a sequenced drop route on signing in and then follows the round throughout the shift. This approach opens up a range of agility options to create better alignment of load to resources. Potential benefits of this approach include:

- Carrier no longer needs to be committed or constrained to a learned route

- Opportunity for dynamic flexible routing

- Creates the possibility for different length rounds

- Increased opportunity for division of labour between preparation and delivery.

Whilst these areas are all interesting, it should be noted that whilst driver-/carrier-management applications are perceived as attractive, there are some legitimate reservations around implementation implications and potential impact on driver compliance and labour turnover. In owner–driver models, there is a need to balance entrepreneurial responsibility with control and in the letter environment there needs to be caution that the opportunities for agility created by the technology remain consistent with attractive employee value propositions and socially responsible contracts. The technology is an enabler and not a determinate of the nature of labour agility.

Finally, an emerging area of interest is using the mobile as a delivery mechanism for e-learning with training materials being made available through 'app-based' technologies which enable user authentication, interaction and certification of completeness. There are significant cost benefits with this approach for a distributed workforce.

CUSTOMER INTERACTION

Perhaps the greatest opportunity for mobile will be for more integration with the delivery receiver through mobile networks.

CORE APPLICATIONS

The basic interaction is around proof of delivery captured on the hand-held device. This will continue to be the main application as the market moves increasingly to tracked parcels as the norm. However, this is now merely a market standard with no competitive advantage – the more significant competitive applications will be in other areas.

- An area which has developed significantly is customer communication before delivery through the receiver's mobile. This interaction enables receivers to either confirm or choose an alternative delivery time or nominate an alternative delivery location, which then increases first-time hit rates and reduces expensive failed and second-delivery processes, whilst also increasing receiver and merchant satisfaction.

- Dynamic interaction can be extended through the driver contacting the recipient once the item is in transit to inform of delays or even, in one application, enabling the driver to make a delivery to the individual if they are near rather than at the destination address. Clearly, this type of customisation will be price-determined.

- Posts are developing receiver apps, which bundle a range of functionality to increase communication with the post, which can include delivery preferences, alternative addresses, return services and tracking capabilities. Again, the goal is to increase the visibility of information in order to rationalise and increase the success of both collection and delivery operations.

- A less standard area being developed is for the delivery company to take on a deeper role in managing customer interaction for the merchants, acting as either a sales point of related goods for the merchant or as a customer-service point, monitoring customer satisfaction. The mobile provides the platform for this service.

Other applications which have been considered have been use of customer mobile with one-off authentication pins to provide identification for high-value goods and the development of cash-collection systems using card readers on the hand-held device. In these cases, there is clearly a trade-off between operational efficiency and increased income.

Interaction with the customer either to drive delivery efficiency or to increase the value of the visit will become an increasingly important part of the postal mobile story.

LEVERAGING THE INFRASTRUCTURE

An area which stimulates interest but has yet to be developed is to determine if and how a post can identify additional revenue opportunities through data gathering which would increase the value of the delivery route and support overall profitability. Other opportunities which have been mentioned include: monitoring traffic and street-furniture conditions; business-location verification; smart-meter reading; mapping information and property-related services.

CONCLUSION

The use of mobile technology in its widest sense is becoming an important and integral part of operating in intelligent delivery organisations. The visibility and distribution of information through mobile networks and devices between receivers, merchants' systems and carrier operations' systems will be a fundamental component of building agile productive companies.

Early-adopting posts, with a vision and direction for intelligent use of mobile technology as an integral part of their operational mix, will be best practice and become the benchmark in this area. The end picture of the mobile-enabled post is not yet clear but the need to engage in creating one is more than proven and apparent.

QUESTION FOR THOUGHT AND DISCUSSION

The opportunities to explore and develop interesting and productive applications of mobile technology seem to be unlimited. Should posts only develop those applications which directly increase profitability, or improve service or customer interaction; or should they allow and encourage innovations which may not have any immediate positive business benefit?

The future consumer expects a flexible service centred on their individual needs for delivery and these needs will change from customer to customer and from day to day.

EMERGING TECHNOLOGIES AND OPERATIONAL PLANNING

Michael Faltum
PostNord

INTRODUCTION

Given a marked decline in letter volumes year by year and with paper-based products challenged by an ever-increasing substitution by electronic solutions, it becomes paramount to have a technology plan for the entire organisation as well as for all products, machines and production IT.

The Engineering Department at PostNord Danmark has for the past seven years issued an annual 'Technology Plan' with a catalogue of new postal technologies that have become available. At management level, this catalogue is used as an inspiration for developing new postal services and for issuing enhancements to the production set up.

POSTAL TECHNOLOGY

In the last 100 years, postal technology has undergone three major evolutions:

- The first one was when we changed from walking and riding on horseback to using bicycles and trucks.

- The second evolution was in the '60s and '70s when we introduced outward sorting by machines resulting in the construction of the first postal-factories for mail sorting.

- The third evolution emerged in the '80s and '90s when we introduced sorting by machines to the mail carrier's route.

Despite not changing the way mail was handled as seen from the customer's point of view, in their own right each of these milestones were giant leaps forward for the postal business. The improvements were local and they only affected the internal workload and routines in the distribution offices and sorting centres. The input and output was not changed, nor was the net result. Unsorted mail entered, it was processed in a combination of manual and mechanical routines, and it was delivered to the receiver by the local mail carrier as the very last process.

Now we face the fourth evolution: smart mail. The decrease in mail volumes, new digital trends and – more importantly – major changes in our daily way of living call for new ways to utilise a modern postal service. In the future, the postal service will be seen as a necessary add-on to our daily activities like purchasing something on the Internet or getting groceries delivered at our doorstep.

This calls for a new way of thinking. We must minimise internally our production cost in order to mitigate the drop in mail volumes and we still have to optimise the use of production equipment in order to reduce costly manual labour. At the same time, we have to improve our quality levels to meet new market demands.

However, our most important focus must be on the consumer. It is crucial to become more agile and stop thinking in terms of parcels, flats and letters. We have to recognise that in the consumers mind, they are all the same: mail!

The consumer expects us to handle their mail in a flexible manner and meet their individual needs for delivery. The best part is that demands will most likely change from day to day in the future. The future consumer expects a flexible service centred on their individual needs for delivery and these needs will change from customer to customer and from day to day.

In short, the postal service of tomorrow must adapt and respond to the modern way of living.

NEW CHANGING DEMANDS

The management of postal companies will have to face these new changing demands in the coming years. Many decisions must be taken based on market requirements and the need to adapt quickly to new service requirements. In general, the way the postal business works must be reinvented.

Decisions are taken top down and head on. Postal companies must first ask 'What is needed?' and then 'How can it be done technically?' In order to facilitate strategic technical decisions in PostNord Danmark, the Engineering Department continues to issue the annual 'Technology Plan' – currently released in its seventh edition.

The plan falls into three parts. The first part is a short status update on ongoing projects, while the third is a summary list of the expected lifetimes of running equipment. The most interesting and comprehensive part, however, is the second, which is a catalogue of emerging new technologies. It lists new technologies spotted by the engineering department during conferences, exhibitions, meetings with vendors and from monitoring research projects carried out to explore new emerging production techniques.

This method of listing and presenting new technologies, in a structured and orderly fashion, has enhanced the development of several new services. One example is the common sort-plan manager for all products and routes.

A NEW SORT PLAN

The ADMSPM sort-plan manager from Siemens was chosen as the future sort-plan editor and sort-plan manager in Post Danmark in 2007. The ADMSPM was initially implemented for letter sorting and the first step towards a unified and centralised system for generating sort plans was taken.

In 2011, when the decision was taken to go for full sequencing of flats in Denmark, all major systems were already in place. Due to its modular design, ADMSPM could easily be extended also to handle flats. However, the NEC machines used for sorting flats at PostNord Danmark were never designed for full sequencing, so a semi-automatic system had to be developed in order to introduce sequencing of flats.

The new system draws on the ADMSPM to make the NEC machines capable of printing a six-digit sequenced number on each flat. Based on this number, the letters can subsequently be manually sequenced in universal sorting shelves. The manual part of the sequencing now only requires sorting according to the printed numbers. Staff members do not have to read any addresses or sort according to shelves marked up by street names and house numbers.

The sequencing is done entirely by numbers. Thus, the sequencing can be done either centrally or locally without any need for specific knowledge of local route layouts. The net result is that speed can be improved even though the sequencing is a manual task.

PostNord Danmark has still not implemented full integration between parcel distribution and letter distribution. However, plans exist for connecting the parcel sorting to the system. This will allow the route planning to be common to all products and it will make way for implementing a single unified hand-held terminal for the last mile.

WHAT'S IN THE FUTURE?

With the future smart mail, the sender and receiver can be in full control of the delivery. One day the mail can be delivered to the home address, the next day to the office and on Friday to the summer cottage, should the receiver decide that the weather in the weekend will be perfect for a stay in the countryside.

In the coming years, the consumer will expect to be able to have online control of the delivery and to be able to add additional services directly from a smartphone or a tablet connected to the Internet.

Smart mail calls for a new layout in production. In the future, a postal company will not be able to claim it has 20–25 mail-sorting centres distributed evenly around the country each taking care of its own slice of the country. In order to utilise the new services, the factories will still have to be distributed evenly around the country; but technologically they will all be clustered as one giant factory. Conceptually, there will be only one (virtual) factory covering the whole country, but physically subdivided into 20–25 real factories.

These factories must all produce according to one centralised sorting scheme regardless of the type of mail, and they must all use the same back-end for sort plans, OCR reading and video coding. They must all adhere to one common layout of transportation routes and to one nationwide layout for the last mile.

All schemes and layouts are expected to change dynamically. If the mail volume is low on a Monday, five sorting centres might be closed down for the day, and the sorting has to be distributed evenly among the rest. The sorting schemes, transportation routes and the last mile must be automatically and dynamically changed accordingly.

The fact that the consumer expects to be able to control the delivery of their personal mail, and to be able to buy additional services, calls for the post to track each and every mail item in order to honour the changes to the very last minute – even after the sortation has started.

CONCLUSION

In order to be prepared for these new challenges, the post has to look beyond the horizon. New technologies, never before known to the postal industry, have either to be implemented directly or to be adapted for the future needs in the postal business.

This calls for a broader mindset. In the coming years it will be a prime task for engineering departments to present new technical solutions to the management level at a scale and speed never before seen, and to ensure that the solutions present viable opportunities for the business.

At PostNord Danmark, Engineering has always tried to keep an open mind towards new technologies. On several occasions, it has paid off to keep an eye on other production branches as well, spotting new techniques that can be adapted to the postal industry.

Presenting a catalogue of emerging new technologies in the annual 'Technology Plan' has proved valuable, and several new technologies once described in the plan have directly or indirectly led to enhancements in production or to new products or services.

QUESTION FOR THOUGHT AND DISCUSSION

Having their engineering department take the responsibility of examining and presenting new technologies for upper management has proven to be a success within PostNord Danmark. Is it the responsibility of engineering departments to set the stage for the technological evolution of postal organisations? When reinventing the post, where should the initiatives come from?

SECTION 4
CHANGING THE CULTURE OF POSTS

Derek Osborn

When reinventing the post, identifying new strategies for the changing market, putting new leaders in place and changing the operations are all tough challenges but nevertheless *relatively* easy compared to changing the culture. Culture is about 'the way we do things in our business or organisation', the habits, behaviours and attitudes – in other words, it is our organisational ethos or DNA – what makes us who we are.

It is hard enough to change the culture of any organisation but for many businesses in the postal industry, this means changing the organisational 'habits' that have been deeply ingrained for centuries and which may have been suitable for other times but are now no longer fit or sufficient for the modern market environment. Traditional, hierarchical, monopolistic-thinking, bureaucratic, risk averse and slow to change or adapt are some ways to describe the typical rigid, compliance culture of the un-reinvented post. By contrast, responsiveness to customers, engagement of staff and longer-term strategic behaviour are cultural components that posts will want to aspire to develop and migrate towards.

Dr Sascha Hower and **Lily Loo** outline the journey to customer-centricity on which Singapore Post has embarked. They outline the imperative to focus on customers in the highly competitive markets in which posts now operate. They show that it is important to understand the customer experience and their expectations, but also to harness social media, which is becoming increasingly significant. To change the culture requires more than a policy shift: a whole new mindset is needed to ensure that every employee 'lives and breathes' customer value.

Kristina Survilé continues this theme of employee engagement and why it is so important. Engaged employees are going to be more effective, more committed and more concerned about customers and quality – as well as the longer-term success of the business. There is also a strong link between good staff engagement and the loyalty of both employees and customers. Developing this kind of engagement culture is not easy but, as Lithuania Post learnt from their experiences, motivation is key and it is influenced by having the right kind of incentives.

Dr Eva Savelsberg and **Ute Simon** challenge postal and parcel operators to be more strategic and think longer term, to be better prepared for an unpredictable future. For many, the culture in the postal sector has been to focus mainly on short-term planning and tactical approaches, rather than on the longer-term investment planning that is necessary in order to build flexibility into systems and operations. This kind of planning agility is needed now and in the future, if posts are to adapt to changing market needs whilst still maintaining efficiency and profitability.

Dr Christoph Beumer makes another case for strategic behaviour – this time for longer-term engagement with customers, focusing on the total value of ownership in order to build stronger and longer-term customer partnerships. This is in contrast to a prevailing culture of chasing quick gains and the next quarterly sales or income targets and so building sales figures without fostering sustainable customer relationships. There are many opportunities for posts to develop more strategic partnerships, both with customers and suppliers, which can shift the focus from cost or price to *value* and shared investment for future sustainability.

…we recognised the need to change the way we engage and serve the customer. We needed to take an holistic approach to customer service and transform mindsets across the whole company.

CUSTOMER-CENTRICITY: CORE POSTAL DNA FOR A HIGHLY COMPETITIVE E-COMMERCE MARKET ENVIRONMENT

Dr Sascha Hower & Lily Loo
Singapore Post

INTRODUCTION

Modern technology and the rapid pace of innovation have changed our lives forever. For the postal world, this has resulted in a swift decline in letter mail and a sharp rise in parcels and packets due to e-substitution and the growth in online shopping globally.

Do postal operators still have a place in this new environment, which is characterised by new norms in customer expectations for transparency, speed, choice, convenience, reliability and more?

The answer is obvious as we look around us and see postal peers reinventing themselves to adapt to the changing landscape. It is clear that, in order to survive, postal companies need to transform to meet the changing needs of the customer. What is even more evident is that the playing field is now much wider, with non-traditional providers competing with traditional postal players for market share in delivery solutions.

Let us take a look at the impetus for postal companies to make customer-centricity core to their DNA in a highly competitive e-commerce market. We present these insights with some specific examples from Singapore Post's customer-centric journey.

WHY IS CUSTOMER-CENTRICITY CRUCIAL FOR POSTAL COMPANIES?

Four major trends have changed the postal landscape in recent years and they have a major impact on how posts interact with their customers.

1. DECLINING LETTER VOLUMES IN MORE LIBERALISED MARKETS ARE A THREAT TO THE TRADITIONAL POSTAL BUSINESS MODEL

Electronic substitution of physical letters is a global trend. UPU research shows that in 2012 worldwide letter volumes came down by 3.5% or approximately 12 billion items compared to the year before. In the last decade, the letter-related revenue in industrialised countries has come down by around 20% but still accounts for more than half of the revenues of the postal players.[1] This significant letter-volume decline across the world has led to a need to find alternative sources for growth.

In addition, continued liberalisation of postal markets increases the need to offer customer-centric solutions to maintain high market share and not lose it to new market entrants.

2. B2C E-COMMERCE PARCELS HAVE THE POTENTIAL TO FORM THE BACKBONE OF FUTURE BUSINESS MODELS – BUT THE MARKET IS MORE COMPLEX AND HIGHLY COMPETITIVE

E-commerce is now increasingly becoming one of the core pillars for many postal operators in both developed and developing countries. Forecasts for online retail development becoming a key driver for B2C parcel growth are around 10–11% p.a. for the next 5–10 years.[2] This is so even for mature markets like the UK and Germany, while for developing countries like India the projected growth rates are much higher with a CAGR of more than 30%.[3] Such growth forecasts excite and attract competition from many players: postal players, the big integrators, major regional parcel players and many small local players fight for the same customers. In addition, major e-commerce companies have extended their offerings downstream, providing their own parcel delivery services.

In this highly competitive environment, excellent customer experience becomes a key differentiator.

1   Koch, D., Consumer spend on postal services rises, *Union Postale*, No. 4, December 2013, p.17
2   Lierow, M., Sarrat, M., & Janssen, S., Delivery Logistics for European E-Commerce, Oliver Wyman report 2013, p.2
3   Kakroo, U., E-Commerce in India: Early birds, expensive worms, McKinsey report 07/2012, p.1

3. IN A B2B4C ENVIRONMENT, E-COMMERCE HAPPENS WITH MULTIPLE CUSTOMERS FOR ONE TRANSACTION

Whereas posts have always been operating in a B2B4C environment, customer expectations both from sender and receiver are much higher in a competitive e-commerce environment.

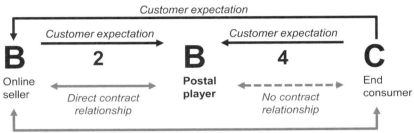

'Free next-day delivery' has become a norm in many markets, masking the fact that delivery to the end consumer accounts for a significant part of the logistics cost in the online selling market. Delivery providers are uncomfortably 'sandwiched' between the online seller (contractual partner) and the end consumers who readily complain if service is below their expectation. They feedback to both the delivery party and the online seller, and even further afield as well – in online blogs, for instance.

Again, excellent customer experience – for the 'B' and the 'C' customer – becomes a key differentiator in this setup.

4. HARNESSING SOCIAL MEDIA FOR CUSTOMER ENGAGEMENT

In the past, capturing the 'voice of the customer', to know what our customers are telling us, their requirements or feedback on our products or services, may have required study methods such as focus groups, individual interviews or survey/ analysis of conventional call drivers. With the evolution of social media, one significant change is that the customers have their own voice, one that can be heard 'rapidly, loudly and frequently' via social media. Social media significantly amplifies the effect of poor customer experiences. Widely used social platforms, like Facebook and Twitter, allow end consumers to broadcast unsatisfactory or unpleasant customer experience in real time and with the powerful potential to go viral. If not managed well, the negative sentiments of any single individual could severely damage the reputation of the overall service quality of a postal operator.

When designing its Customer Service strategy, it is imperative that a post has a Social Customer Engagement strategy, to manage and respond to customer feedback and safeguard overall brand perception.

HOW DOES SINGAPORE APPROACH CUSTOMER-CENTRICITY?

With the transformation of Singapore Post into a regional champion for e-commerce logistics and trusted communications, we recognised the need to change the way we engage and serve the customer. We needed to take an holistic approach to customer service and transform mindsets across the whole company.

WE MADE CUSTOMER-CENTRICITY OUR DNA, A CRITICAL STARTING POINT

In early 2013, the company reviewed its corporate values and subsequently identified five values as critical for a company actively transforming into a regional e-commerce logistics player. One of these was 'Total Customer'. This value requires everyone to be fully committed to our customer – and in the complex e-commerce B2B4C environment, 'customer' now takes on a broader meaning.

The table below illustrates how Total Customer means looking at all stakeholders and all the end-to-end interactions. Only when tackled comprehensively can all the interdependencies be managed smoothly.

B 2	**B** 4	**C**
With online sellers	Internally	With end consumers
(1) **Meet customer needs** e.g. clear product and service features	(4) **Ensure excellent performance** e.g. stellar operations & customer service	(7) **Offer c-centric solutions** e.g. 24/7 parcel lockers, easy returns
(2) **Deliver on your promise** e.g. on-time delivery, minimal loss cases	(5) **Know your customers** e.g. proactive, integrated CRM	(8) **Engage with (unhappy) customers** e.g. active social-media interactions
(3) **Make performance transparent** e.g. daily automated performance reports	(6) **Build a customer -centric organisation** e.g. 'Total Customer' ' mindset across post	(9) **'Surprise' the end consumers** e.g. deliveries on New Year's Eve

WE ADOPTED AN HOLISTIC APPROACH TO IMPROVING CUSTOMER EXPERIENCE

To help its employees live the Total Customer value, Singapore Post launched the C3 (Customer-Centric Culture) programme. C3 is an organisation-wide change-management programme with an holistic approach that aims for every individual in the company to embrace this value. The holistic approach is also about the customers, so they will experience that value through our employees when they transact with us. Led by the Vice President of Customer Excellence, the C3 programme focused on developing in its people a conscious mindset and behaviour change to ensure that service becomes second nature. *The customer* needs to be at the centre of all decisions. The cornerstone of the C3 programme is to provide our customers with solutions that are *'Accessible, Reliable* and *Easy-to-use'*, as reflected in the service slogan *'We A.R.E. SingPost'*.

More than S$100 million has been invested into enhancing our customer-service proposition, including modernising postal infrastructure, rolling out 24/7 services, mobile solutions and company-wide service training.

WE USE A P-E-E-R STRATEGY TO HELP EVERY EMPLOYEE LIVE THE 'TOTAL CUSTOMER' VALUE

Employees of Singapore Post were put through a comprehensive change-management programme. Using the P-E-E-R strategy, the programme rolls out initiatives to help every employee live out the 'Total Customer' value, focusing on:

- *Preparing* the mindset of employees to be customer-centric

- *Engaging* employees frequently, seeking their inputs on how the company can be more customer-centric

- Providing tools as *Enablers,* to facilitate the journey and track improvement, and

- *Rewarding* exemplary customer-centric behaviour.

To prepare employee mindset, Singapore Post worked with a training partner to roll out a series of service training programmes. Powered by the Disney Institute, this is one of the best-in-class when it comes to delivering a good customer experience. At Disney, when the dishwashers were treated to a banquet, served on sparkling clean crystal dinnerware, they saw for themselves how their work contributed to the overall customer experience. Through a customised programme, every SingPost employee, from delivery personnel to the back-office finance assistant, sees his or her role as providing the overall customer experience and takes pride in doing the job well.

One key success factor in our journey is top management's constant engagement across all employee levels. From quarterly *Leadership Conversations*, where the thought processes of the senior leadership are shared and aligned, to regular *Breakfast with the CEO* meetings with the front liners, management finds opportunities to hear from the ground directly. Members of the executive leadership team also take on the roles of courier, postman, telemarketer, post-office counter staff and phone agent for a day, in the *Let Us Do the Job Together* initiative. By being at the frontline themselves, senior leadership gets to understand the customer issues first hand, so the customer experience becomes one prime object of their decision making. Middle managers are also included in this engagement. For instance, they go out to post-office outlets to help out as Service Ambassadors during the year-end peak periods.

Switching from an 'inside-out' to an 'outside-in' approach, Singapore Post adopted the Net Promoter Score (NPS) methodology for its Voice of Employees and Voice of Customer Surveys. According to the research behind NPS, engaged, loyal employees reduce costs, improve productivity and come up with more creative ideas.[4] Survey results of companies that adopted NPS support the argument that we cannot create loyal customers without first creating loyal employees. Stores that regularly rank in the top group of customer NPS also rank high in employee NPS, and vice versa. Since happy employees make happy customers, we want to track the level of employee engagement and its impact on customer engagement. Although still in an early stage of implementation, initial results of our Voice of Employee 2013 already point to a high awareness of customer-centricity. Employees ranked their highest satisfaction with the way they view themselves and their colleagues living the 'Total Customer' value.

Throughout the year, exemplary instances of service are recognised and rewarded. In line with the Disney service training programme, an 'all expenses paid' learning journey trip to the nearest Disney theme park will be awarded to deserving employees who consistently exhibit customer-centric behaviour.

---

4   Reichheld, F., & Makey, R., The Ultimate Question 2.0, 2011, p.185

CUSTOMER-CENTRICITY ALSO MEANS OFFERING CUSTOMER-CENTRIC SOLUTIONS

Whilst, on the one hand, the C3 programme prepares, engages and enables employees to live the 'Total Customer' value by rewarding them when they exhibit such behaviour, the service slogan 'We A.R.E. SingPost' focuses on getting business units to work on changing customer and business processes to deliver solutions that are **A**ccessible, **R**eliable and **E**asy-to-use.

Some examples include:

a. Our POP Stations (24/7 parcel lockers) were made *easier to use* when we expanded the range of services from just picking up and posting parcels, to parcel returns, card-on-delivery payments and many more. They are also made more *accessible* to the customer when the average distance between lockers is just 3.5 km. With more lockers in the pipeline, this distance will reduce to 2.5 km by the end of 2014.

b. We now offer a reliable one-stop e-commerce solution based on an integrated IT infrastructure comprising web services, order management, warehouse management, carrier selection and booking, POP Station integration, returns management and multi-lingual customer support at affordable rates. Since its launch in early 2013, many e-commerce brands have already come on board this *reliable* and *easy-to-use* B2B4C solution.

c. vPost, our home-grown international shipping service, makes it possible for customers to buy online from merchants across the USA, including those that do not ship internationally, and have them delivered right to their door step. This service is now made available to Australia, India, Malaysia and Thailand. In addition, vPost customers enjoy a new repacking service, where items are repacked into smaller boxes so that customers save on shipping costs. vPost service is now more *accessible* and *easy-to-use*; indeed, we provide globe shopping without globe hopping!

CONCLUSION

With extensive network access and last-mile delivery advantage, postal players across the world are in a good position to support and benefit from rising e-commerce and the resultant logistics needs.

However, a key ingredient for success – and indeed, a necessity for the business to remain sustainable – is customer-centricity. Customer-centricity has to become the core DNA of posts.

Having embarked on the customer-centricity journey, we can confirm confidently that the SingPost Group has benefited significantly from a more empowered group of employees and steady revenue growth. Pursuing customer-centricity is a continuing journey that requires constant review and adaptation. However, it is a journey that we must take if we want to stay in business. In fact, in order to survive the onslaught of changes in the postal landscape, we advocate that every postal business should make customer-centricity an absolute priority.

QUESTION FOR THOUGHT AND DISCUSSION

The imperative for a business to provide a good customer experience is very clear to everyone and we are all consumers. So why is it that 'the customer' does not take central place in many postal companies? What needs to happen in order to begin the journey that SingPost has embarked on?

Ultimately, the success of any company depends on the people working for it and their attitude, as well as their levels of effort and engagement.

DEVELOPMENT OF SERVICE AND QUALITY IMPROVEMENT CULTURE

Kristina Survilė

AB Lietuvos paštas

INTRODUCTION

In a complex, competitive and changing environment it is becoming harder to run profitable businesses in a traditional way. When existing possibilities for optimisation of processes and costs are fully exhausted, there is still an opportunity to foster greater productivity, innovation, excellence and quality by developing a service and quality improvement culture. Ultimately, the success of any company depends on the people working for it and their attitude, as well as their levels of effort and engagement.

Postal companies usually employ huge numbers of people and are amongst the biggest employers. However, it is difficult to develop a culture that fosters improvement, engagement and commitment to quality – it does not occur naturally. Companies have to work hard to achieve this.

ADVANTAGES OF ENGAGED EMPLOYEES

It is common in postal companies to find a large proportion of long-term employees who have worked there for many years, who have been with the company for 20, 30 or more years. It would be good to believe that the majority of them are really committed to the company but, increasingly, loyalty and engagement have much less to do with their length of service.

Equally, employees can be devoted to the company but lack initiative or enthusiasm to do more than is expected and make additional efforts for the company. On the contrary, engaged employees are loyal and committed to the company, emotionally bound to it and make discretionary efforts to do their best in performing tasks and helping the company reach its goals and be successful. Engaged employees care more about what they are doing, they are more productive, less likely to leave, they give better service and generate higher profits.

Employee engagement is crucial in service businesses where people constitute the main asset of the company and service quality is a key factor for success. Engaged employees can make positive changes in the whole value chain, leading to greater efficiency of operations, reduction in operational losses, growth in quality level and customers' satisfaction, and increases in revenue, profit and total shareholder returns.

A direct relationship exists between employee satisfaction and customer satisfaction. A smile, a greeting, care and additional help for the customer represent a high quality of service that cannot be easily measured. Even on a customer service call, the customer can feel as if someone is smiling at the end of the phone (or not) and truly cares about their concerns. Opinions of customers depend heavily on the kind of attention they receive and how they are valued, which is a direct reflection on how they are treated by company employees.

This kind of customer perception can be more important than good advertising as it relates to direct experience of the service provided and reveals the company's attitude towards the customer. If customers feel that they are served well by the staff, who are doing their best to please them – then they will show their loyalty to the company by coming back and recommending it to others. If not, they will not come back and will probably deter others as well. Thus customer loyalty comes directly through the company's engaged employees.

HOW TO ENGAGE EMPLOYEES

Only those employees who are happy with their work, rewards and relationship with the management can engage with the company and contribute effectively to the company's wellbeing. According to research conducted in 2012 by the Hay Group[1], employee engagement has a negative trend in the whole world and the

---

1   Source: 20 March 2014 forum, 'Employee engagement: how to transform it to results', presentation by Eligijus Kajieta, Manager for Baltic nations, productised services at Hay Group

turnover of employees is increasing. One of the challenges corporate executives face today is to maintain motivated and engaged employees. Although it might seem that it is impossible to transform a demotivated employee into a passionate one, there are many small actions that can be taken to turn an ordinary workplace into a more engaging environment.

The starting point would be to understand why employees do not perform as expected. Do they have the necessary qualifications, tools and skills to be able to give a good service? Do they understand why they are doing certain operations, or the nature of the organisation's vision and mission? By dedicating enough time to explaining the meaning of their work to employees, the company helps them to feel more engaged and fulfilled, and encourages their initiative to work with individual style and to yield better results for the organisation.

The development of an 'employee-engaging culture' begins at the top of the organisation. Leaders and management play a key role in the engagement of employees. But having engaged managers does not guarantee that staff will also be engaged. If management enjoy their good position and all the benefits it gives but lack respect or a fair attitude towards employees then it will be difficult to maintain motivated employees.

When rules are introduced by the company and employees are expected to follow them, then the same rules should be observed by the management. When building trust among employees, it is crucial to have the same standards for the whole workforce and for all levels of managers. Employees cannot be obliged to be engaged with the organisation – it is something they give as part of their discretionary behaviour if they trust their managers and can feel that they are being treated fairly, and that their opinion matters and is valued. It is a two-way relationship between the employer and employee.

Offering material rewards in return for their discretionary efforts is one of the ways to incentivise employees. However, there are many ways to show employees that they are valued and a simple acknowledgement, a 'thank you' or other kinds of recognition, can make the employee feel appreciated. Reward and recognition programmes that challenge employees to excel are one way to boost employee engagement.

The development of a business with a caring and employee-engaging culture is about building trust, fairness and integrity – these are the essential components of the quality of interaction between management and employees.

DEVELOPMENT OF AN 'EMPLOYEE-ENGAGING CULTURE' AT LITHUANIA POST

The Financial Services Department of Lithuania Post provides evidence that good leadership and employee engagement work. Three years ago, the major players in the financial services market did not consider Lithuania Post to be a serious competitor. Its financial services looked outdated, having a monopolist's attitude towards clients and generating revenues that were several times lower than those of competitors.

The changes started with the new leader. When introducing herself to the company, the new manager of the financial services unit said that she was always inspired by stories in which someone had a vision and concentrated on their work in order 'to turn deserts into blooming gardens'. Three years ago, the situation at financial services looked like a desert – a small market share, inconvenient services and unattractive working conditions. But the new leader had a vision and ambition to turn the desert into a blooming garden.

The first steps taken were to improve the 'what' and the 'how'. Existing processes in the area of financial services were examined and re-engineered – what it was possible to do at once was done immediately; the rest was taken into an action plan for the future. Front-office staff were trained to provide good customer service and they were also trained in selling techniques and methods. The outcomes of these actions were: simplified processes, reduced service-provision time, more attractive services to clients, and staff with additional selling skills.

After this stage, Lithuania Post expanded its network with 200 PayPost outlets each with one or two working places exclusively for financial services. Financial services are now provided at post offices and PayPost outlets. The only difference between the two service-provision networks is the style and methods of personnel management. The personnel at PayPost outlets are managed by the Financial Services Department and personnel at post offices are managed by Postal Network Division. As the Postal Network Division has a broader range of services, processes, post offices and employees, it is less flexible in management and all processes take more time. Due to its greater flexibility, the Financial Services Department was able to be the first to start developing a service and quality improvement culture within the Financial Services Division.

The Financial Services Department put the main focus on giving support to front-line employees and the 'why' was emphasised. Everyone in this department is working to support front-line employees who directly provide services to the customers. Front-line manager–supervisors regularly (once a month) visit PayPost operators personally. Besides their routine review of operations and compliance with procedures, front-line managers spend time talking informally to the employees about work issues, problem solving, the latest changes and reasons why certain actions were necessary and why certain outcomes were distributed in a certain way. Explaining and sharing knowledge and information take place through dialogue and employees have an opportunity to express their opinion and to discuss it. This form of support and the open discussions generated trust in the management, which turned into greater commitment to the company.

With this development of an organisational climate that enhances employee engagement, the Financial Services Department has reduced education requirements for newly hired front-office employees. As Lithuania Post now has its own training programme, a university degree is no longer a must. We were pleased to notice that new employees have good ambition, cherish their work and are better motivated.

The Financial Services Department also changed its reward system for employees working at PayPost outlets: the new reward system emphasises sales of the most profitable services. Bonuses are now given for meeting targets in sales and quality. The same amounts of money are given as previously, but the fact that they are now awarded for different reasons has made a difference. The previous motivation system gave bonuses by default to all front-line employees except those who did not reach personal goals. Psychologically, default bonuses were accepted as part of the regular salary and therefore bonuses taken away were considered a penalty. This system worked more as a demotivator rather than as motivator. The new reward system has no default bonuses. Bonuses are given individually every time the personal goals are met (instead of taking individual bonuses off for unmet goals).

With the same processes, tools and resources but two different approaches to front-line employee management, we now have a different level of employee engagement. It is also pleasing to note that the greater level of employee engagement has led directly to better financial results!

CONCLUSION

The company benefits from having engaged employees as this results in increased efficiency of operations, quality of services and customer satisfaction – and the positive outcomes these generate. But engagement is not a constant matter or something that occurs by accident. Moreover, employee engagement has a negative trend in the wider world and it is thus a continuing challenge for management to maintain an engaging environment.

Employee engagement starts with top-management engagement and it takes time and effort to build trust, fairness and integrity between management and employees, which are the key components for an engaging culture. While developing business strategies and making plans for the future, management should take action to support employee engagement and develop a quality-improvement culture.

QUESTION FOR THOUGHT AND DISCUSSION

Who is responsible for employee engagement at your company and how is employee engagement managed?

Since those strategies imply long-term investments, the real artistry lies in not preventing any future ability for agility and adaptability…

A GLANCE INTO THE FUTURE OF POSTAL AND PARCEL LOGISTICS

Dr Eva Savelsberg and Ute Simon

INFORM GmbH

INTRODUCTION

Are you facing unpredictable times? Parcel volumes have increased dramatically over the last decade due to the e-commerce boom and yet, despite serving a growing market, parcel operators are still competing fiercely. Moreover, there is no universal approach for them to adopt in order to get the most benefit from this evolving market and to strive for excellence.

During many high-level strategic discussions with parcel operators from all over the world, specific challenge patterns become obvious. These challenges can be answered if appropriate strategies aimed at quality, efficiency and sustainability are pursued. Since those strategies imply long-term investments, the real artistry lies in not preventing any future ability for agility and adaptability.

DIFFERENT SCENARIOS AND STRATEGIC POSSIBILITIES

So what are these possible scenarios and what approaches are available to answer those challenge patterns without limiting your strategic possibilities in the future?

The three key challenge patterns are:

- Increased quality pressure whilst ensuring cost efficiency

- Increasing social demand for sustainability

- Changes in service patterns.

These challenge patterns are not only affected by market developments but also by the planned evolution of the specific operating company.

INCREASED QUALITY PRESSURE WHILE ENSURING COST EFFICIENCY

Around the globe, postal and parcel operators have very different strategies regarding their logistic centres – their size, their geographic distribution and the way they are managed. In order to reflect changes in the overall postal landscape, the individual logistics concept will probably change over time. In the beginning, postal and parcel operators develop their presence in a country by starting with a few parcel centres and some connected depots for distribution over the last mile.

Then with a growing customer base and better area coverage, they might change their strategy and enlarge their infrastructure as well as exploit additional areas. Then they might go for some bigger parcel centres or a higher number of medium-sized centres. At a later stage, the company might decide to operate with their own discreet network – with big and medium-sized hubs and smaller depots.

In order to be competitive and to expand their market share during those evolutionary stages, it is important for operators to be able to manage this landscape of diverse logistics centres at its best. To ensure service quality at an ambitious cost level, it is essential to make most efficient use of the transport network and transport equipment. Finally, the exchange of relevant data between logistics centres and within a transport network has to be target oriented, so that all relevant data is available for all participants at the right time.

INCREASING SOCIAL DEMAND FOR SUSTAINABILITY

The public demand for a company's operations to be sustainable is omnipresent: postal operators have to improve their green footprint demonstrably by reducing their overall CO_2 emissions. Furthermore, in the context of an increasingly competitive labour market, the motivation and engagement of employees has become more and more of an issue recently. This is especially the case in Germany, where a lot of companies are already challenged by demographic changes, and it is hard to find qualified employees and then retain them, depending on where the company is located. Therefore, it is essential for postal companies to develop a strong long-term human resourcing strategy.

CHANGES IN SERVICE PATTERNS

Considerations regarding service patterns often revolve around two major decisions: make-or-buy or make-and-sell. After a decade of outsourcing services, insourcing of supporting services seems to be a favourable strategy again. Other strategies in this context are to offer own infrastructure and logistical services to customers and to engage in third-party logistics.

The key questions for postal and parcel operators are: what can we do today to best prepare for those future challenges and how can we plan for the future with more confidence?

BUILDING BRIDGES INTO THE FUTURE

Companies must avoid getting 'stuck' in today and instead be able to build planning bridges into the future. In this context, software can be a good enabler that allows a company to prosper today whilst also preparing for the future. IT systems can support postal and parcel companies to manage today in the most efficient way as well as to build a bridge from today into an unpredictable future. To illustrate the potential of software and what different system components are able to achieve, consider the following example of two fictitious countries called 'Postalia' and 'Postonia' (see Figure 1).

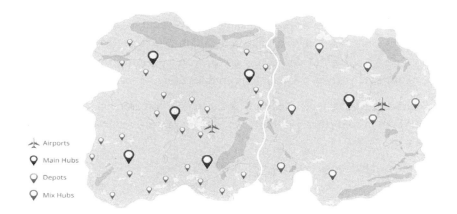

Figure 1: Postalia and Postonia

Different conditions in the two countries lead to different strategic concepts. In Postalia, the postal company chose to build bigger hubs that distribute mail and parcels to depots, which then serve specific areas. Whereas Postonia has one big central hub combined with several medium-sized hubs for re-sorting and serving the last mile.

HUB MANAGEMENT

A smart software system has to support those various concepts in an appropriate way, taking into account the different characteristics of all logistics centres (e.g. different layouts, specific customers, geographical representation, different equipment, special processes such as returns handling or bulky goods).

Main hubs or air hubs, for example, are usually the heart of the network: coping with a high transport volume and a high complexity, they are the engine of the company's supply chain. Therefore, a system with a high level of automation and optimisation is needed that supports the precise business processes of a specific hub. Intelligent management software for this type of hub needs to take into account all logistics processes on the premises and inside the sorting centre in order to improve the efficiency of those processes considerably. The same applies to medium-sized hubs, even though they have a lower transport volume and reduced complexity: intelligent management software that supports their individual level of automation and optimises all yard-related processes will achieve improved transparency, a better traceability and superior KPIs. In smaller depots with standardised processes, the demand is again different: even though they need some level of automation, there are fewer turnovers, the overall complexity is rather low and optimisation is not needed. Therefore, a software approach adjusted to the overall typical needs of the depots of a specific company limits the occurring costs while offering transparency and an improved handling on the premises.

To analyse the impact of intelligent optimisation software on yard handling, INFORM compared three different yard-management approaches in a hub simulation:

- Manual handling

- Rule-based decision-making software

- INFORM's yard-optimisation software, SyncroTESS.

The results show that manual handling usually works well in a small hub because the transport situation is not that complex and an experienced dispatcher is able to handle all logistics processes in a satisfactory manner. If the transport volume increases, however, and the overall situation becomes more complex, the efficiency of manual yard handling suffers drastically.

Therefore, deploying a software system would be a suitable approach for bigger and more complex centres to enhance handling efficiency. However, a rule-based system that rigorously follows specific if–then rules will often not react in the most appropriate way for any given situation. As INFORM's hub simulation shows, strictly rule-based software can even worsen the overall efficiency. In order to really increase hub efficiency and improve KPIs dramatically, intelligent optimisation software is needed that takes all logistics processes on the premises and inside the sorting centre into account, considering all relevant constraints and behaving in a situation-responsive manner.

Comparing KPIs of the hub simulation emphasises the superiority of intelligent yard management software over the alternative yard-handling approaches: the average service time for inbound trailers can be cut by one-third. At the same time, the overall travel of shunting vehicles is significantly reduced, especially compared to manual handling but also compared to rule-based decision making. Moreover, the changeover times for inbound and outbound gates are lowered so that the throughput can be increased accordingly.

Achieving a lot more with the same amount of resources is an important aspect of intelligent management software. Moreover, the simulation shows that even with a reduced number of internal shunting vehicles, more turnovers can be realised when using yard-optimisation software (see Figure 2).

Simulation Outcome
- reduced average service time for inbound trailers
- lower overall travel of shunting vehicles
- lower changeover times for inbound and outbound gates
- increased throughput
- reduced number of shunting vehicles
→ Do more with less

Figure 2: Benefits of intelligent yard-management software

The implementation of an intelligent management system also has a positive effect on employees' working conditions as it leads to a considerable increase in transparency and a more gratifying working life, enabling the dispatcher to concentrate on strategic and special tasks or unexpected events. By creating new areas of responsibility, employees are relieved of routine tasks, supporting them in driving up productivity.

The simulation results emphasise in an impressive way that investing in intelligent optimisation software today lays the foundation for postal and parcel operators to achieve flexible growth in the future.

BENEFITS FOR CROSS LINKING

In a network of main hubs, air hubs, medium-sized hubs and depots, all sites have to be effectively linked with each other to create the corresponding synergies. Here again, software offers important benefits for cross linking covering the following aspects:

- Network planning
- Transport optimisation
- Asset management.

NETWORK PLANNING

With network-planning software, companies can review their current and planned transport network by testing different scenarios. This enables them to identify bottlenecks and peaks within their transport network early on. A smart software tool helps postal companies to streamline their network and to reduce transport costs, emission or transport lead times. Even though some of these goals are dependent on each other, business cases demonstrate significant reductions.

TRANSPORT OPTIMISATION

As far as transport optimisation goes, software solutions should support tactical planning as well as real-time optimisation. While tactical planning is done several times throughout the day, real-time optimisation flexibly adapts to changed circumstances during transport execution. To support real-time optimisation effectively, a comprehensive GIS functionality and track and trace of all transports should be in place. With regards to tactical transport planning, INFORM rose to a challenge (with live operational data) against dispatchers known to be masters of their profession. Although experience and smartness can produce amazing results, the challenge proved that one cannot compete with advanced algorithms.

ASSET MANAGEMENT

Even though passive transport units are comparatively small, they can be quite expensive and transporting them throughout the country can be a costly matter.

With asset-management software, these units can be managed in an intelligent way, resulting in a much lower total number of units while still covering peaks, avoiding stock outs and optimising their availability throughout the entire network.

Having a smart network which optimises not only transport movements but also the resources and equipment used for transport enables the postal operator to maintain the right balance between service level and cost efficiency. Moreover, it leads inevitably to a significant reduction of CO_2 emissions by utilising the entire network far more efficiently and eliminating unnecessary travel.

CONCLUSION

With uncertain conditions and an unpredictable future, postal and parcel operators worldwide can overcome some of the key challenges they are currently facing if appropriate strategies aimed at quality, efficiency and sustainability are adopted. For this, intelligent software plays a decisive role in not limiting the company's future ability for agility and adaptability. The most important requirement for software is that it needs to be flexible and adjustable to the business strategy and evolution of a post or parcel operator. It has to be adjustable in terms of adding functionality or interfaces for evolving infrastructure reasons as well as having whole software packages in place, like asset management, in order to enhance further business developments. Smart systems do not only increase the company's efficiency but can also add to employee motivation and improve the company's green footprint demonstrably. For this, a reliable partner is needed, supporting them in choosing and facilitating the right strategy for a prosperous and sustainable future. INFORM solutions enable postal companies to be better prepared for unpredictable times and to look into the future with confidence.

QUESTION FOR THOUGHT AND DISCUSSION

Intelligent systems can clearly help to manage and plan transport networks more efficiently, allowing for more agility in short- and long-term horizons; but what other variables and dynamics need to be taken into account when managing complex systems?

Companies should take into account more than just overall operating costs if they want to be competitive in the long term.

TOTAL VALUE OF OWNERSHIP FOR A LONG AND STRATEGIC CUSTOMER PARTNERSHIP

Dr.-Ing. Christoph Beumer

BEUMER Group GmbH & Co. KG, Beckum, Germany

INTRODUCTION

Companies should take into account more than just overall operating costs if they want to be competitive in the long term. An integrated approach is far more important. By looking at the Total Value of Ownership (TVO), the effectiveness of business investments can be described more comprehensively, from the right perspective and therefore more meaningfully. It is important to include economic as well as ecological and social aspects when developing machines and systems, as the BEUMER group does, making it not just a supplier but a strategic partner for postal and CEP companies.

PRESSURES ON POSTAL AND CEP COMPANIES WORLDWIDE

The pressures on postal and CEP companies in a competitive environment are increasing. Not only must they save costs but they must also reduce environmental impact and respond to influential market trends. These include new technologies, the increasing use of new sales channels such as e-commerce – which raises high customer expectations for immediate deliveries – and also growing globalisation. As a result, the demand for more efficient sortation and distribution systems continues to grow throughout the world.

For example, the gross domestic product in many countries in Asia is steadily increasing which, in turn, is leading to an increase in wages. This is particularly noticeable in China and India. A new middle class has come into being which is significantly changing the consumption patterns of the population in developing countries. The volume of trade is increasing and purchasers are demanding ever-shorter delivery times. This is also affecting the working environment, for example in distribution centres (or hubs). Here too, it is becoming necessary to think and act more globally, whereas the local orientation of such service providers is reserved for niche markets. Postal and CEP companies must therefore be able to adapt flexibly and dynamically to changing requirements in order to survive in the marketplace.

INVESTMENT FOR IMPROVED COMPETITIVENESS

The trend towards automation continues to be important for the survival of service providers and is therefore strongly increasing in distribution centres. Material flow technology is becoming more complex and systems must be able to carry out more flexible tasks or be adapted to suit changing local situations. Highly efficient processes are required to enable parcels to be dispatched to customers quickly.

For example, e-commerce and mail-order companies have recently also been offering products which, up to now, had been difficult to transport automatically because of their dimensions. However, the automation of existing solutions or the integration of new machines and systems is usually accompanied by significant costs for the user. To enable them to make these strategic investment decisions in a targeted manner, companies must analyse all direct and indirect costs in advance in order to calculate the Return on Investment. In doing so, they should set their sights on more than just the procurement and operating costs.

To enable companies to work efficiently, their machines and systems and the associated production processes must be directed towards long-term customer benefits. That's why we develop all solutions with an integrated approach, the Total Value of Ownership (TVO). While the Total Cost of Ownership (TCO) exclusively takes into account the economic aspect of a product, TVO is based on and includes ecological aspects such as energy-saving operation or resource-conserving production as well as social factors. Examples of these include sorters which run very quietly and therefore produce only a small amount of vibration. This makes for a more pleasant working atmosphere and less noise pollution.

The systems also simplify the sorting of goods of all kinds, and this is carried out automatically instead of by hand. This enables our customers to describe the effectiveness of their business investments holistically and more meaningfully. Companies are not only able to determine their direct costs but, above all, the 'Total

Value' of the solution to be supplied over its entire operating life. For this purpose, we identify three interacting factors: market developments, risk management and longer-term sustainability.

ADAPTING FLEXIBLY TO INCREASING DEMANDS

To enable companies to convert flexibly or adapt their machines and systems, for example to accommodate changes in consumer behaviour or to adapt to trends such as the increasing use of e-commerce, we collaborate with the users to work out which solution is able to accomplish the required task and whether it will also be capable of meeting future requirements. The decisive factor here is whether performance can be increased without also increasing the costs in the long term, such as in the case of inefficient sorter drives or if maintenance is frequently required.

An important point is therefore the availability and usage of machines and systems that have been supplied and installed. Malfunctions and machine shutdowns frequently lead to long downtimes, especially in intralogistics. Production and delivery can come to a complete halt. Possible risks must be clearly identified, analysed and evaluated. As a strategic partner therefore, we take care of our customers from the initial project meeting to the running system and beyond. As part of this service, we offer flexible agreements, an efficient supply of spare parts and comprehensive training for users of our systems. As an example, these agreements can include upgrading of the systems by our customer support staff as soon as new sorting technologies and software controllers are introduced. It is important to us not only to rectify faults, but also to help companies to satisfy future performance and technology demands. For example, as the mechanical parts of a sorter wear out over the years, staff must respond immediately at the first signs to prevent possible consequential damage. We are in a position to offer high system availability over the whole working life. Our objective is always to make processes even smoother in order to ensure a value-added material flow.

The third factor relates to sustainability. This subject, in particular, represents a particular challenge for intralogistics. In order to find a clear answer to the question of sustainability of a system, machine or drive, we have developed a validation system in the form of the BEUMER Sustainability Index (BSI). We use this to measure sustainability systematically and continuously on every new machine and also on existing solutions. Each of the three levels – economic, ecological and social – is divided into five categories for evaluation purposes using the BSI.

These include 'efficiency and effectiveness', 'lifetime', 'operating costs', 'production-related raw material consumption' and 'training and development standards'. These categories are evaluated with up to five points. The total of these is used to provide a classification into the levels 'excellent', 'very good' and 'suitable for improvement'. If a product is classified as suitable for improvement, we subject it to reengineering to ensure that it achieves a higher level.

DESIGNED FOR GROWTH

Our product base includes modular high-performance sorting systems, which enable widely varying goods – such as parcels, products in bags and bulky goods – to be sorted, distributed and checked in large quantities quickly, reliably and accurately. For example, a customer who wanted to fulfil his global commitment to sustainability and environmental protection in his distribution centre through efficient sorting technology also approached us with a requirement for fast and accurate sorting. We installed our energy-saving Cross Belt and Tilt Tray Sorters. After all, most of the energy in this centre was used in operating the sorting and conveyor equipment. Because our solutions use linear synchronous drive technology, the energy consumption is 75% lower than that of sorters with conventional technology.

The process here is sophisticated. Workers place the boxes with the products from the warehouse on a conveyor belt. This takes them to an in-line sorter, which transports the parcels to one of three possible positions, depending on whether the goods are to be dispatched in batches or mixed in newly assembled boxes. At one station, boxes are sent directly to the dispatch sorter. Another station receives boxes that contain items in certain batches, which are then sent to the in-feed unit of the pre-sorter. The third station is designed for boxes containing items that are brought together for mixed deliveries. These are delivered directly to the warehouse, where workers remove the items from the boxes and place them on shelves. They can then be taken as required and placed in plastic trays on the conveyor system. The conveyor transports the trays to a further conveyor on Level 2 of the building. The trays and the boxes with the batches are brought together and emptied. Workers place the items on the Cross Belt Sorter. This automatically sorts the goods from the plastic trays into defined containers, which are discharged in the tilt area. From here, they are transported by a system of conveyor belts to the workers, who place the items manually on the final sorter, a Cross Belt Sorter. The chutes are equipped with batch divider flaps. These are activated when a complete batch has been delivered. The batch is thereby isolated and can subsequently be packed in a box by the operator. The box is pushed onto a roller conveyor, which transports it to the Tilt Tray Dispatch Sorter. We have integrated the system and device controllers for the machines seamlessly into the user's warehouse management system. This prevents bottlenecks and the customer achieves faster throughput.

CONCLUSION

We have entered into a three-year service contract with the customer to enable us to offer maximum operational reliability. As part of this agreement, service engineers are stationed on site, with responsibility for the support and preventative maintenance of all material flow equipment and for management of the local spare parts stock. This agreement also includes upgrading the systems when new sorting technologies and software controllers are introduced, which illustrates how Total Value of Ownership can be more important than just the cost of the equipment.

Thanks to the sorting systems and software controllers used, the distribution centre works more efficiently than conventional installations. The company has also achieved a number of important objectives, including greater operational efficiency, flexibility and freedom from errors on dispatch. The handling costs and the energy costs have decreased, and the environmental impact of the operations has also been reduced.

QUESTION FOR THOUGHT AND DISCUSSION

The concept of Total Value of Ownership (TVO) has been introduced here in the context of the supply and maintenance of sorting machines and systems – are there other areas of the postal industry where this concept, along with strategic partnering, could play an important part in securing long-term business sustainability?

SECTION 5
CHANGING THE WAY THE POSTAL SECTOR IS GOVERNED

Edited by Graeme Lee

Sunflower Associates

In this section we have three interesting topics regarding governance of the postal sector. Until recently, governance was not an issue since the status quo of the postal sector was never in question. National postal operators were either departments of government or state-owned corporations with a generous monopoly to compensate for providing the universal service. But in recent years, market liberalisation, competition, technology and changing customer demands have all had major impacts on the sector.

Market liberalisation in Europe in the late 1990s was a major catalyst for change, with a requirement for national and European regulation of the postal sectors. The opening of the European postal market led many countries to question the traditional model of governance of the national postal operator. Greater commercial freedom for the national operator was seen as a prerequisite for them to compete in this newly liberalised environment. However, few governments provided the ultimate commercial freedom of privatising the national operator, as if privatisation was a line not to be crossed.

Perhaps technology will have the greatest impact on how the postal sector is governed. Dramatically falling letter volumes first question and will later threaten the concept of universal service. The 'one size fits all' of an obligation to provide universal five- or six-day delivery to every home in a national territory will disappear in the not-too-distant future. Some countries have already reduced the number of deliveries per week or moved to community boxes to reduce the unit cost of delivery. That is not to say operators will not provide five-, six- or even seven-day delivery, but only in commercially viable areas. Regulators will have to be more dynamic and flexible in the way they regulate the postal sector to ensure service provision matches actual demand.

Are the countries that are currently privatising their national operators secretly wishing they crossed the 'privatisation line' prior to market liberalisation? Did liberalisation dilute the value of the national operator by upsetting the balance between reserved area and universal service obligation? Are regulators acting quickly enough to take into account changing customer demands in the postal sector?

Carla Pace opens the section by reviewing the reasons behind the recent spate of privatisations of European postal operators. Focusing on three recently privatised operators and three more that are in the process of privatisation, Carla looks at the rationale for privatisation. Several privatisations have been driven by a requirement for governments to reduce national debt and Carla questions whether the 'forced' sale of those operators might be a blessing in disguise.

Steve Hannon follows with an in-depth look at the privatisation of Royal Mail in the United Kingdom. First considered almost 20 years ago, the privatisation has been mired in politics from all sides which has prevented an earlier sale. Steve looks at the 20-year history and the factors that finally allowed the sale to take place. The sale was massively over-subscribed, leading to accusations that government had undersold the national asset.

Closing the section, **Juan Ianni** considers the efficacy of the traditional definition of universal service for posts. He asks if the time is right, given falling mail volumes, liberalisation and rapid changes in technology, for universal service to be reconsidered. Juan asks also if it would be more appropriate to consider whether a 'basket' of services should be considered within the scope of universal service that could be provided through postal or other networks.

...governments have been incentivised to define and commit to privatisation plans in order to obtain financial assistance from international partners...

EUROPEAN POSTAL PRIVATISATIONS AND THE ECONOMIC CRISIS

Carla Pace

Cullen International

INTRODUCTION

A new wave of IPOs has affected European postal markets in the current two-year period. In 2013, shares in bpost, Royal Mail and CTT, the Belgian, British and Portuguese postal incumbents respectively, were offered to the public. Further postal privatisations are expected in 2014: Poste Italiane, the Hellenic Post ELTA and the Romanian Post.

This is quite a concentration of public sales compared with previous activity in the sector. Privatisation of postal incumbents in Europe in the twenty-year period to 2012 consisted of only four IPOs (the Netherlands, Germany, Malta and Austria), and two direct share sales (50% minus one share of the Belgian incumbent and 22% of shares in the Danish Post).

The usual economic arguments justify old and new privatisations alike: promote efficiency, open access to capital markets for investments and enable the operators to react faster to market changes. However, although some of the 2013–2014 sales appear to have been on the cards for several years, it is notable that recent preparations came to a head within the context of the current economic and sovereign debt crisis, with these latter factors playing a key role in accelerating the pace of postal privatisations.

PRIVATISATIONS IN EUROPEAN POSTAL MARKETS

Between 1994 and 2012 the postal incumbents of the Netherlands, Germany, Malta, Austria and Belgium were privatised.

Country	Postal operator	Privatisation process
NL	Post NL	• IPO of 30% of shares of the company (at the time, KPN combined both the postal and telecoms incumbents) in 1994 • Process completed in 2006 when 100% of shares of the company, now renamed TNT, became private
DE	Deutsche Post	• IPO of 29% of shares in 2000 • Public ownership gradually reduced in the following years
MT	Malta Post	• 35% of shares sold in 2002 to Transend Worldwide (subsidiary of New Zealand Post), which later sold its shares to Redbox Ltd (subsidiary of Lombard Bank) • Privatisation completed with an additional 25% sale of the state's shares to Redbox Ltd and the public quotation of the remaining 40% of shares on the Malta Stock Exchange in 2007
AT	Österreichische Post	• IPO of 49% of shares in 2006
BE	bpost	• Sale of 50% minus one share of the company (named at the time La Poste/De Post) to a consortium of Post Danmark and the British private equity fund CVC Capital Partners in 2006 • Danish Post withdrawn in 2009 due to its merger with the Swedish Post, leaving all the non-public shares in the hands of CVC • Further privatisation in 2013 (see Table 2)

Note: In 2005, 22% of Post Danmark's shares were sold to CVC. The equity fund sold back its shares to the Danish state in 2009 when Post Danmark merged with the Swedish incumbent Posten AB to form the company now known as PostNord AB (owned 60% by the Swedish government and 40% by the Danish government).

Sources: Annual Reports, company and government websites

Table 1: Postal incumbent privatisations between 1994 and 2012

After a few quiet years, postal-sector privatisations began picking up again in 2013, when shares of three postal incumbents were offered to the public (bpost in Belgium, Royal Mail in the United Kingdom and CTT in Portugal).

Country	Operator	Date	Actual proceeds	Resulting ownership
BE	bpost	21 June 2013	€812m	• 50%+488 shares Belgian state • 49.54% free float • 0.46% bpost staff • Note: the IPO carried on the privatisation process started in 2006. A part of the 50% minus one share in the hands of the private partner CVC was offered to the public. CVC sold its remaining 19.67% shares in December 2013.
UK	Royal Mail	11 Oct 2013	£1.7bn (€2bn)	• 52% retail and institutional investors (33% and 67% respectively) • Royal Mail staff 10% • UK government 38% • Note: the privatisation of Royal Mail was mentioned in the first Hooper report in 2008, defined in the Postal Act 2011 and included in the Coalition Programme of the current government[1].
PT	CTT	5 Dec 2013	€520m	• 56% institutional investors • 30% Portuguese State (via Parpública, the state-run management holding company) • 12.62% general public • 1.38% CTT staff

Sources: Company websites, press clippings

Table 2: Postal incumbent privatisations in 2013

Further postal privatisations are expected in 2014 in Italy, Greece and Romania:

---

1   Hooper, R., 'Modernise or decline – Policies to maintain the universal postal service in the United Kingdom', December 2008; Hooper, R., 'Saving the Royal Mail's universal postal service in the digital age – an update of the 2008 independent review of the postal services sector', September 2010; Postal Services Act 2011, Chapter 5, Part 1; 'The Coalition: our programme for government', May 2010

Country	Operator	Date	Expected proceeds	Announced % of shares on sale
IT	Poste Italiane	2014	Between €4bn and €4.8bn	• IPO of up to 40% of shares to retail, institutional investors and staff
GR	ELTA	2014	n.a.	• Sale of 39% of shares
RO	Poşta Română	Before 30 Oct 2014	n.a.	• Sale of 51% of shares

Sources: Press clippings, institutional websites

Table 3: Expected postal incumbent privatisations in 2014

Three of the countries involved in the recent wave of privatisations are involved in international financial assistance programmes (Portugal, Greece and Romania). Italy, which has not required external financial assistance, nevertheless has the second-largest debt-to-GDP ratio in Europe after Greece.

INTERNATIONAL FINANCIAL AID AND PRIVATISATION PLANS

The unprecedented global financial crisis of 2007–2008 and the consequent economic downturn brought about the deterioration of public finances and significant increases in sovereign debt levels across the world.

Euro-area member states, in particular Greece, Ireland and Portugal, were at the centre of the recent European sovereign debt crisis. Eight[2] countries in Europe had to ask for financial assistance from other EU members and international institutions in order to preserve their own financial stability, and that of the EU and the overall euro area. Different financing mechanisms have been made available to address these problems[3].

---

2   Ireland, Greece, Spain, Latvia, Hungary, Portugal, Romania and Cyprus: see European Commission Directorate General for Economic and Financial Affairs (DG ECFIN) website, http://ec.europa.eu/economy_finance/assistance_eu_ms/intergovernmental_support/index_en.htm.

3   The stabilisation mechanism set up in May 2010, initially composed by the European Financial Stabilisation Mechanism (EFSM) and the European Financial Stability Facility (EFSF), was integrated in October 2012 by a permanent rescue mechanism for euro-area member states, the European Stability Mechanism (ESM). Alongside these measures, funding from the International Monetary Fund (IMF) and possible European Central Bank (ECB) purchases of sovereign debt on secondary markets are also available. Further, Balance of Payments (BoP) assistance is also accessible for member states that have not yet adopted the euro. Source: European Commission DG ECFIN website, http://ec.europa.eu/economy_finance/assistance_eu_ms/index_en.htm.

The financial assistance provided predominantly takes the form of loans, conditional on agreement to, and compliance with, a strict macroeconomic adjustment programme (macroeconomic conditionality). Should the recipient country fail to make progress in line with the recommended measures, the financial assistance could be suspended. The privatisation of state-owned assets is one of the elements that may be included in adjustment programmes, not only for the expected efficiency improvements that might be achieved for state-owned enterprises but also because their proceeds contribute to relieving government debt.

It is thus clear that governments have been incentivised to define and commit to privatisation plans in order to obtain financial assistance from international partners and/or to reduce fiscal stress.

FISCAL STRESS PROVIDES ADDITIONAL REASONS FOR PRIVATISATION

PORTUGAL

Portugal requested international financial assistance in April 2011. The Economic Adjustment Programme (EAP) negotiated between the Portuguese authorities and the troika – composed of the European Commission (EC), the European Central Bank (ECB) and the International Monetary Fund (IMF) – included a joint financing package of €78bn for three years aiming to reduce the gross-public-debt-to-GDP ratio in the medium term. Among other measures, the EAP involved the privatisation of some of the most important state-owned companies, including the postal incumbent CTT[4]. On 5 December 2013, following the approval of the legal framework necessary for privatisation[5], the government privatised 70% of CTT's shares, selling 56% directly to institutional investors and the remainder to the general public and CTT staff[6]. According to a statement from the Ministry of Finance, around 90% of the proceeds (~€468m) were used to repay public debt[7].

---

4 Among other assets considered: ANA (Aeroportos de Portugal), the waste-management company EGF, and the national air carrier TAP.

5 Decree 129/2013 of 6 September 2013

6 See   http://www.ctt.pt/fectt/export/download/investidores/press_releases/Full_Year_ results_PT.pdf (situation at December 2013)

7 See http://www.publico.pt/economia/noticia/governo-usa-90-das-receitas-com-a-venda-dos-ctt-para-abater-divida-publica-1618866

GREECE

Greece has been receiving financial support through an EAP since May 2010. A second EAP was approved on 14 March 2012.

The release of disbursements is subject to the positive evaluation of progress made with respect to specific policy criteria. In particular, the privatisation of public companies is expected to boost efficiency in the economy and to contribute to the reduction of public debt, including from lower subsidies and other transfers or state guarantees to state-owned enterprises[8].

Within this framework, the Greek authorities have committed to proceed with a large privatisation plan[9]. The Hellenic Republic Asset Development Fund (HRADF) was established on 1 July 2011 to contribute to the overall recovery and growth of the Greek economy, maximising proceeds from the development and/or sale of state-owned assets whose property has been transferred to the Fund, including the voting rights of ELTA[10].

Currently, 90% of the shares of the postal incumbent ELTA are held directly by the Hellenic Republic, with the other 10% owned by TT Hellenic Post Bank (privatised in 2006). The government announced its intention to sell 39% of its ELTA shares on 18 September 2013.

According to the privatisation plan detailed in the latest memorandum of understanding[11], the regulatory framework required for ELTA's privatisation is being put in place. A ministerial decision to determine the exact content of the universal service has already been taken, while the compensation mechanism for the universal service provider has been drafted and pre-notified to the EC, DG Competition. Further clarifications and amendments requested by the EC are now being processed by the Hellenic Republic and ELTA.

ROMANIA

Romanian authorities requested financial aid from the EU and the IMF for the first time in Spring 2009, in order to deal with risks related to the country's balance of

---

8   Third review of the second economic adjustment programme for Greece (July 2013) and Memorandum of Understanding update 7 December 2012

9   The specific measures that the country has to implement are foreseen in a Memorandum of Understanding.

10   See HRADF website: http://www.hradf.com/en

11   Annexed to the third review of the Second Economic Adjustment Programme for Greece (July 2013), Table 9.1, p.193

payments[12]. The new measures that came into force on 4 July 2013 will continue to support the economic programme of the Romanian government, aiming to consolidate macroeconomic, fiscal and financial stability[13].

The further privatisation of the Romanian postal incumbent, Poşta Română, was already included in the structural reforms listed in the memorandum of economic and financial policies[14] presented by the Romanian Government to the EU and IMF for the previous 2011–2013 balance of payments precautionary assistance programme. The main shareholders of Poşta Română are currently the Romanian state (75%) and the Proprietatea Fund (25%). In December 2012, the government announced its intention to sell 51% of the shares of Poşta Română in 2013. Interested investors were requested to prove they had available at least €150m for a cash injection into the company's share capital. However, no investor came forward, despite the purchasing deadline being twice delayed. Finally, in May 2013, the Romanian government decided to proceed first with a restructuring of the national postal operator and then to re-invite investors to submit offers. On 23 January 2014, the Ministry for Information Society confirmed the extension of the deadline for the submission of non-binding offers to 30 June 2014. The privatisation process should be completed by 30 October 2014.

ITALY

Even in countries where no financial assistance programme is in place, the debt-to-GDP ratio may nevertheless represent a concern for governments.

On 11 December 2013, the former Italian Prime Minister referred to plans for the privatisation of Poste Italiane in a speech to the Parliament. Nine major public companies were included in the privatisation file drafted by the government[15]. In a communication to a Senate Committee on February 2014, the then Finance Minister confirmed that no more than 40% of the shares would be sold via an IPO for retail investors (including Poste Italiane staff, for whom favourable conditions

---

12 http://ec.europa.eu/economy_finance/assistance_eu_ms/romania/index_en.htm

13 Third EU medium-term financial assistance programme and IMF stand-by arrangement, July 2013. The new programme will run for 24 months (until September 2015) and foresees assistance for an amount of up to €2bn from the EU and up to 1.75bn of Special Drawing Rights (SDR) equivalent to about €2bn from the IMF. The financial assistance is expected to be treated as precautionary, with no actual disbursement foreseen.

14 http://ec.europa.eu/economy_finance/eu_borrower/balance_of_payments/pdf/memorandum_28022012.pdf

15 http://www.lastampa.it/2014/03/22/economia/privatizzazioni-il-dossier-di-letta-cpbw2gnIzOCcaWUmCAN6lI/pagina.html

could be set) and/or Italian and international institutional investors during 2014. He also said explicitly that proceeds from the privatisation (expected to be between €4bn and €4.8bn) will be used to reduce public debt, which reached the level of 133% of GDP in 2013[16]. In March 2014, the current Finance Minister, Pier Carlo Padoan, confirmed the government's willingness to proceed with the planned privatisation at a faster pace.

CONCLUSION

The list of privatised postal incumbents is growing quickly in Europe, revitalising the stock-market interest in the postal sector that had remained quiet for some years. 'Classic' economic goals of promoting efficiency, providing access to capital markets and facilitating faster reactions in a dramatically changing market remain valid explanations for this new impulse. However, a clear role in accelerating the pace of postal privatisations was also played by governments forced to plan and react to the current economic and sovereign debt crisis. It will be interesting to see whether the privatisations whose pace has been 'forced' by the economic crisis will prove to have more or less successful outcomes than those whose origins were more protracted.

QUESTION FOR THOUGHT AND DISCUSSION

The 'forced' nature of some of the recent privatisation activity is highlighted here but will this affect the outcomes for these companies? Is the injection of investment and market confidence sufficient to allow these newly privatised operators to flourish in an increasingly competitive market?

---

16   Italian National Institute of Statistics (ISTAT) press release on annual national accounts 2013.

…there has to be a determination by the government of the day to push through the change…

A BIRD'S EYE VIEW OF THE ROYAL MAIL PRIVATISATION

Steve Hannon

PLCWW

INTRODUCTION

In 2013, history was made when Royal Mail – founded over 500 years ago in the reign of Henry VIII – was privatised. Why did this happen? Why did it take so long to happen? More fundamentally, what changes is this likely to promote in the future and what potential lessons are there for other countries and for the wider postal industry?

The privatisation of Royal Mail was first proposed by the Conservative government in 1992. However, this was abandoned following widespread public resistance led by the Communication Workers' Union (CWU) and the Labour Party. Ironically, it was a Labour government that next attempted to privatise Royal Mail in 1998 but internal opposition thwarted the sale. A further attempt by the Labour government in 2009 also failed due to the equity partner not meeting the government's valuation[1].

THE JOURNEY TO PRIVATISATION

The journey to the 2013 privatisation started with the publication of the European Commission's 1997 Postal Services Directive, which established common rules governing the provision of postal services across Europe. This included strict rules on the provision of a universal postal service and liberalisation of the letters market

---

1   Duncan Campbell-Smith, *Masters of the Post: The Authorised History of The Royal Mail*

by the end of 2010. It also required the creation of independent national regulatory authorities and so, in the case of the UK, Postcomm was established in 2000.

Postcomm took an aggressive approach to liberalisation, licensing a number of private companies to collect and deliver mail and enabling them to access Royal Mail's network and, in 2006, fully liberalised the UK mail market. This led to a number of operators entering the postal market and the UK led the way in developing downstream access (DSA) agreements between Royal Mail and other licensees. Royal Mail's competitors now handle 45% of addressed letter mail posted in the UK[2] at the point of posting, although Royal Mail still delivers about 99% of mail[3].

However, of greater consequence has been the impact of digital media on Royal Mail, which has seen the overall addressed-letters market in the UK decline from a peak of 84 million items per day in 2005 to about 50 million per day in 2014 (a reduction of 40%).

These issues contributed to a worsening of Royal Mail's financial position and in 2008 the Labour government commissioned a report by Richard Hooper CBE to examine the future of Royal Mail. The Hooper Report[4] concluded that, in the face of market decline, Royal Mail needed to increase its efficiency, which was estimated to be 40% less than that of its competitors[5]. Indeed, Hooper concluded that inefficiency was a much greater problem than competition for Royal Mail. In addition, the Report identified Royal Mail's pension deficit – at nearly £6 billion, it was at the time one of the largest of any reported by a UK company – as a significant risk. A third issue was poor labour relations, which had seen damaging national strikes in 2007. Finally, the Report was critical of the relationship between Royal Mail and Postcomm.

Hooper recommended that Royal Mail be modernised more rapidly. To achieve this, he recommended a strategic partnership between Royal Mail and private-sector companies with experience of successfully transforming a major business in difficult circumstances. He also recommended that Post Office Ltd. should remain in the public sector and that the government should tackle Royal Mail's historic

---

2   Royal Mail Website, February 2014

3   Presentation of Royal Mail's half-year results for 2013–14, 27 November 2013

4   Modernise or Decline: Policies to maintain the universal postal service in the United Kingdom – An independent review of the UK postal services sector, 16 December 2008

5   Statement by Adam Crozier, Royal Mail's Chief Executive in the 2006–7 Report and Accounts

pension deficit. Finally, he recommended that the regulatory function should be transferred from Postcomm to the communications regulator, Ofcom.

The general election of May 2010 led to a Conservative and Liberal Democrat coalition government which lost no time in including the modernisation of Royal Mail in its programme[6]. Hooper was asked to update his 2008 Report and concluded that little positive had changed:

- The decline in the number of letters being sent was greater than forecast in the 2008 Report;

- Royal Mail's financial position had deteriorated and the pension deficit had increased to about £8bn (as at end March 2010); and

- Despite important steps forward on modernisation, Royal Mail still lagged well behind the leading postal operators[7].

THE POSTAL SERVICES ACT OF 2011

The Coalition pushed forward with legislation and the Postal Services Act of 2011 resulted in the following actions:

- The ability of the government to sell up to 90% of Royal Mail's shares to private investors with at least 10% being offered to Royal Mail staff

- The separation of the Post Office business from Royal Mail

- The government to take over the assets and liabilities of Royal Mail's pension scheme

- The transfer of postal regulation from Postcomm to Ofcom

- The maintenance of a six-day universal service.

Ofcom became the postal regulator on 1 October 2011 and rapidly set about changing regulatory policy. It allowed Royal Mail greater freedom in setting its prices, only price regulating the basic second-class letter price (with a cap of 55p) along with large letters and packets to 2kg. Future price increases over a seven-year period would be limited to the Consumer Price Index (CPI).

---

6   Queen's Speech to Parliament, 25 May 2010
7   Saving the Royal Mail's universal postal service in the digital age, Richard Hooper CBE, September 2010

Ofcom also believed that the best way of preserving the USO was for Royal Mail to be commercially viable, setting a range of 5–10% EBIT[8] as an appropriate target. It also required Royal Mail to improve and sustain its profitability in achieving this target, rather than doing so through price increases.[9]

At the same time, Royal Mail had started a transformation programme focused on two main strategies: first, by improving efficiency and, second, by transforming the focus of the company from letters to parcels to take advantage of the boom in e-commerce. An earlier purchase of German Parcels (later re-christened GLS) in 1999 had proved to be an astute piece of business as this not only enabled Royal Mail quickly to build a European network to support cross-border e-commerce but also provided it with its most profitable business area[10].

In July 2010, Moya Greene was appointed as chief executive. Moya had previously been CEO of Canada Post where she had trebled the company's profits despite falling mail volumes. She maintained the focus of the two strategies as key enablers to getting the company in shape for privatisation.

THE SALE OF ROYAL MAIL

With all the enablers in place, the government announced that the sale of Royal Mail would take place on 15 October 2013. Ten per cent of shares were issued free of charge to Royal Mail's 150,000 employees, with a further 60% being issued as an IPO[11] and the remaining 30% held by government. The sale price was set at £3.30 per share, valuing Royal Mail at about £3bn and raising £2.2bn for the government. The sale was heavily over-subscribed leading to accusations that the government had sold the company too cheaply – some banks having valued the company between £4bn and £4.8bn[12].

So was Royal Mail sold too cheaply? In hindsight, it appears that it was. The share price peaked at £6.18 in December 2013 and, since the sale, the price has rarely dipped below £5.50. Clearly, the government could not afford the sale to be a failure

---

8   Earnings Before Interest and Tax

9   Ofcom – Securing the Universal Postal Service – Decision on the New Regulatory Framework, March 2012

10   In the five years between 2009–10 and 2013–14, GLS accounted for £567m of Royal Mail's operating profits. This represented 49% of the Group's operating profit over this period (all figures exclude Post Office Ltd.).

11   Initial Public Offering

12   *Financial Times*, 6 February 2014

but underestimated the public's desire to achieve a guaranteed return on the first dividend from Royal Mail compared with the paltry returns being received from record low-interest rates elsewhere.

So why did this sale go ahead and succeed following three previous failures?

No sale is going to succeed unless the company being sold is an attractive proposition with good future prospects. Royal Mail had turned a £3m operating loss in 2007–8 into a £440m profit by 2012–13. Royal Mail's transformation programme clearly was a major contributor here alongside the transfer of the pension deficit to the government.

The change in regulator also helped enormously with Royal Mail claiming that under Postcomm it had no control over 80% of prices, whilst since Ofcom's new approach was introduced it has gained the freedom to set over 90% of prices.

The political conditions must also be right. There has to be a determination by the government of the day to push through the change. This was partly enabled by the decision to separate the Post Office from Royal Mail and therefore from the sale (thereby removing some of the political and popular objections that had dogged previous attempts).

Whilst there had been clear support from the management of Royal Mail for previous privatisation attempts[13], this remained a critical ingredient. Moya Greene and her team were clearly on board and worked tirelessly to achieve a favourable result[14].

The decision to award 10% of the shares to employees may also have helped to blunt any opposition from the workforce. Whilst the CWU activated its traditional opposition to privatisation, this was unsuccessful on this occasion. Whilst they did institute a trade dispute with Royal Mail over pay and conditions, the timing of the strike ballot meant the sale had been completed before strike action could take place[15].

---

13   *Masters of the Post*, ibid., p.638

14   *Sunday Times*, 29 December 2013

15   Following negotiations between Royal Mail and the CWU and an agreement entitled 'Agenda for Growth, Stability and Long Term Success' which awarded CWU members a 9.06% three-year pay award from April 2013 to March 2016 along with a number of other commitments regarding future changes.

WHAT NEXT FOR ROYAL MAIL?

So what does the future hold? Royal Mail appears to be well set so far and its latest report showed revenues were up 2%, with parcel revenues (now accounting for 52% of total revenues) up 7% over the previous year[16]. The share price continues to remain between 60% and 70% above its float price, giving the government future opportunities to sell all or part of its remaining 30% share for a high price.

Although Royal Mail claims its transformation programme is virtually complete, it has still further to go on rationalising its mail-centre network and transforming its delivery operation. While it has made strides in improving its productivity, it has not yet closed the 40% gap on its competitors and peers highlighted in the Hooper Report. There will be added pressure from shareholders to improve productivity to raise profitability and, despite members being shareholders, it is likely that the CWU will fight to limit further job losses.

Royal Mail, akin to other universal service providers, also has to face further erosion of its letter market due to digital substitution, DSA operators and end-to-end challenges from TNT[17]. It also faces competition in the parcel market from a host of local, national and international parcel companies. Given the continued growth of e-commerce, including in international markets, it is likely that Royal Mail will act more like a parcel company than a letter carrier in the future.

And what about customers? Larger business customers have always enjoyed an element of price discounting and choice but SMEs and social customers tend to have fewer choices. It is likely that customers will see above-inflation price increases, particularly if Royal Mail fails to close the efficiency gap[18].

So, is privatisation the answer for universal service providers (USPs) elsewhere in the world? Clearly, there are advantages in that it enables the USP to raise capital and act more commercially without needing to seek approval from the government. However, as the case of Royal Mail has shown, it is important that a number of conditions are in place before taking such a step.

---

16 Royal Mail Report and Accounts for the year ending 30 March 2014

17 TNT Post now delivers twice or three times per week in London, Harrow, Greater Manchester and Liverpool as part of a joint venture with LDC (part of RBS). It is also planning to extend to other cities over the next three years, eventually aiming to deliver to 42% of all UK addresses.

18 Royal Mail has announced that the price of a basic first-class stamp will increase by 3.3% and of a second-class stamp by 6% from 31 March 2014. This compares with an inflation rate (CPI) of 1.6% in March 2014.

The maintenance and funding of the USO is the first step. Some USPs believe the USO is a costly millstone whilst others believe it is an advantage, giving it unprecedented national reach. However, funding of the USO is critical to its survival. Many USPs outside Europe still have a reserved area to fund the USO. However, this can distort competition, reduce efficiency and keep prices relatively high. The model in the UK may be a way forward where the regulator allows the USP to set its own price levels (with safeguards) to enable it to be profitable and therefore support the USO from its own profits. Competition is still encouraged to motivate the USP to become more efficient, alongside digital substitution.

There may be a requirement to eradicate a large historic debt or liability, such as pension liabilities. If this cannot be done by the USP itself – for example, through the sale of assets or a suitable (limited) provision from future profits – then it may be that the government has to step in to resolve this issue, as occurred in the UK.

Once this is in place, there is a requirement for the USP to put a plan together to ensure it is a profitable venture going forward. In the declining letters market this probably means a focus on cost reduction. It is also important to put the building blocks in place to take advantage of the e-commerce market – the only part of the postal market that appears to be growing.

Once a strong company has been built, thoughts can then be turned to future ownership. Whilst privatisation, via an IPO, may be attractive in countries where share ownership is widely spread, other options, such as sale to an equity partner or partners or a private parcel operator, may be more realistic options.

CONCLUSION

So what is the future for Royal Mail? Success will probably look like transforming the company into an innovative deliverer of packets and parcels focused on both the poster and the end user, with the natural Internet-fuelled growth more than compensating for continued decline in end-to-end letter traffic. Failure, however, could come from placing too much emphasis on traditional forms of packet and parcel delivery, coupled with an inability to continue to cut costs as letter traffic declines. The theory of privatisation is that shareholder pressure will drive the former to the exclusion of the latter – and clearly, from the share price, investors believe in this theory.

QUESTION FOR THOUGHT AND DISCUSSION

What would Royal Mail be like now had it been privatised in the 1990s? What lessons can be learnt for others from the way that it eventually happened?

...is it time to take a closer look at the age-old concept of universal postal services?

UNIVERSAL SERVICE: THE FUTURE IS NOW

Juan Ianni

IanniPost Consulting

INTRODUCTION

The worldwide economic crisis of 2008–9 and the explosive growth of digital communications changed a postal market that was long considered immutable. From 2006 to 2012, global letter-post volumes dropped by 18% for domestic mail and 27% for international mail.[1] These developments have serious implications for a network industry that depends on the efficient handling of large volumes to keep costs and prices low. It also has implications for our traditional concept of universal postal services. This concept was developed when postal services were the most basic, accessible and comprehensive form of communications. The financial sustainability of this concept also has been based, to a large extent, on reserving a significant portion of the basic mail processed through the postal system for a single, government-designated national operator (or 'universal service provider') allowing this operator sufficient volumes to achieve economies of scale and offset profitable and non-profitable service areas.

Both of these long-held notions are under extreme pressure. Today, the mobile-phone penetration rate stands at 96% globally (128% in developed countries, 89% in developing) and there are nearly as many mobile-phone subscriptions (6.8 billion with a 40% annual growth rate in 2013) as there are people (7.1 billion).[2] Therefore, postal communication can no longer be considered the most universal

---

1   UPU, *Postal Statistics 2012*, available from: www.upu.int
2   ITU, *The World in 2013 – ICT Facts and Figures*, available from: www.itu.int

and accessible communications option. Furthermore, fixed-broadband prices dropped by 82% between 2008 and 2012 while postal costs and prices increased. As new delivery points grow (773,882 in 2013 for the USPS) and volumes shrink, the cost of universal service will continue to challenge the efficacy of the reserved area as a funding mechanism. Postal operators have increased their efficiency, reduced costs and diversified their product portfolios to adapt to this new world. However, the jury is out as to whether, over the longer term, these strategies can offset volume losses and the wave of technological and cultural change in the wider communications market. Therefore, this article asks, is it time to take a closer look at the age-old concept of universal postal services; and if so, how should we proceed?

A TRANSFORMED POSTAL MARKET

Before 2008, it was generally accepted that the dramatic growth of digital communications would dampen some mail volumes, but it was believed that this would be offset by increased business-related mail generated by these technologies. In fact, liberalisation, globalisation and privatisation were thought to have more impact than new technologies in determining the future of the postal sector. This optimistic, glass-half-full view was shattered in 2008 as letter-class mail volumes began to plummet along with the global economy.

The USPS, which alone accounts for approximately 40% of all world mail, was particularly hard hit, losing 25% of its mail volumes and an accumulated $46 Billion USD from 2007 to 2013.[3] Other national operators in industrialised countries (Deutsche Post DHL, Royal Mail, Japan Post, Canada Post Corporation, New Zealand Post) also lost significant volume but utilised their commercial flexibility to minimise financial losses.[4] And while e-commerce-driven parcel volumes grew during the recession and continue to do so, fierce competition in this market limits its contribution to universal service maintenance. Furthermore, over the long term, volumes for basic letter-post items will inevitably decrease and, in ten years, may be half of what they were at their highest point in 2006. Economic recovery has slowed the pace of these losses; however, it has not and will not replace the volumes lost, indicating that the traditional link between GDP growth and postal

---

3   *USPS Annual Reports to Congress, 2007–2009*

4   Accenture, *Achieving High Performance in the Postal Industry – Accenture Research and Insights 2013*

volumes may no longer be valid.[5] The 2006–2012 transformation of the postal market represented not simply a loss of volumes, but rather a permanent shift in the fundamentals of the communications market.

POSTAL RESPONSE

In response to these challenges, postal operators have reduced costs and diversified their portfolios by:

- *Narrowing the postal 'footprint'.* National operators are reducing their networks and outsourcing their retail functions to reduce costs. Deutsche Post DHL and TNT Post (Netherlands) essentially eliminated their official post-office networks and now offer access through the retail networks of other service providers.

- *Digitising postal networks to get closer to customers.* Competition from digital media along with evolving expectations has forced postal operators to tailor their products to individual customer needs. Digital mailboxes, parcel lockers and shops, same-day delivery, SMS notification of delivery, 'hybrid' mail delivery options and a host of other, digitally driven applications give customers more control over when and where they receive their mail. Many operators also utilise postal networks as platforms to intersect with other financial, business and government platforms to add value and lower network costs.

- *Diversifying vertically and horizontally.* Postal operators are modifying their business models to move up and down customers' value chains, particularly in the parcels/logistics area. They are also diversifying horizontally by arranging alliances and acquiring equity stakes in other postal and logistics operators – for example, DHL by Deutsche Post, TNT by the national operator of the Netherlands, and DPD by La Poste. ECT's (Brazil's national operator) strategic partnership with Banco do Brasil allows Banco to be present in 95% of Brazil's municipalities, 2,000 of which were previously not covered.[6]

---

5   The UPU estimates 2012 losses of letter-post mail of 4.7% and 4.0% for 2013. 'Development of postal services in 2012... a few preliminary figures', available from: www.upu.int

6   www.correios.com.br; *ITU/UPU, ICTs, new services and transformation of the Post*, Bern, Geneva, 2010

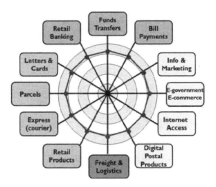

Figure 1: Postal diversification

- *Exploiting growth in parcel traffic.* The e-commerce-driven parcel business is estimated to grow to $1 trillion USD by 2016 and may well determine the future of the postal industry.[7] National operators are working to expand their presence in this fiercely competitive market.

- *Privatising.* Some national operators, such as those of the Netherlands, Malta and Lebanon (through a concession arrangement), are fully privatised, while others, including those of Austria, Belgium, Germany, Great Britain, Malaysia, Portugal and Singapore, are partially privatised. In general, the postal sector has lagged far behind the telecommunications sector in levels of private investment, in part due to the heavy financial burden placed on national operators through the USO.

- *Relaxing USO requirements.* National operators are increasingly asking regulators to reduce the number of delivery days (e.g. USPS and New Zealand Post) and converting expensive door-to-door delivery into less-costly delivery to community mail boxes. As stated in a recent report by the consulting firm Accenture, 'The apparently indisputable universal service obligation is also beginning to show signs of wear and tear as strategies to lower costs begin to affect longstanding regulatory requirements.'[8]

---

7   Considering just national operators, global domestic parcel traffic (99.1% of all traffic) grew by 36% from 2001 to 2012. The rise of the e-commerce-driven parcel market overwhelmed parcel shippers in the US when they were not able to meet delivery commitments during the 2013 holiday shopping season.

8   Accenture, *Achieving High Performance in the Postal Industry*

WILL THIS BE ENOUGH?

Are these improvements enough to ensure future postal universal service viability in a fully digitised world? While progress has been made, there are still valid reasons for concern. First, as liberalisation continues, competition within the postal market will increase, placing more strain and costs on universal service provision. Secondly, technical developments may raise even more challenges for the postal market. One potential challenge is the growth of mobile banking. The mobile-money M-PESA system was introduced in Kenya in 2007; by 2013, it was being used by 17 million individuals, the equivalent of two-thirds of the adult population and now handles around 25% of Gross GDP.[9] Countries such as Kenya may well leapfrog the bricks-and-mortar phase of banking along with the mail such institutions generate. Finally, basic mail volumes will continue to decline and become more costly, eventually making universal service as we know it today unsustainable.

Does this mean that a meaningful universal postal service cannot survive? Not at all, but it does mean that we must start to consider the fundamentals of this service and see how it can be adapted to new realities. Otherwise, we may risk relegating the postal sector to a 'sunset' scenario similar to newspapers and book stores.

HOW IS 'UNIVERSAL SERVICE' DEFINED?

The UPU's Universal Postal Convention defines universal service (Article 3, para 1, Doha Decisions) as follows:

> In order to support the concept of the single postal territory of the Union, the member countries shall ensure that all users/customers enjoy the right to a universal postal service involving the permanent provision of quality basic postal services at all points in their territory, at affordable prices.

Paragraph 2 of the same article provides individual countries some flexibility in implementing universal service:

> With this aim in view, member countries shall set forth, within the framework of their national postal legislation or by other customary means, the scope of the postal services offered and the requirement for affordable prices, taking into account both the needs of the population and their national conditions.

---

9   *Economist*, 27 May 2013. M-PESA is now also offering loans and savings products and has extended to Tanzania, Afghanistan and India.

For purposes of comparison, the ITU Acts state that (Article 3.2) 'Member States shall endeavor to ensure the provision of sufficient telecommunications to meet the *demand* [emphasis added] for international communications services.'[10]

More detail is provided in Article 5, paragraph 37, which says that member states shall endeavour to ensure provision of:

> c) at least a form of telecommunications service which is reasonably accessible to the public, including those who may not be subscribers to a specific telecommunication service...

IS UNIVERSAL SERVICE TRULY 'UNIVERSAL'?

The concept of universal postal services was developed to bring coherence to the exchange of international mail and to facilitate the creation of a unified, worldwide postal territory. However, there are wide variations in the 'universality' of this system.

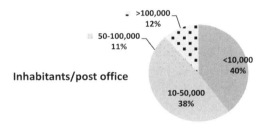

Figure 2: Average population per office for national operators

Most national operators in the industrialised world and the former Eastern Bloc have fewer than 10,000 inhabitants per post office.[11] Conversely, Sub-Saharan countries average 71,389 per post office and 21 countries have over 100,000 inhabitants per post office, some ranging as high as 600,000. There are similar disparities in delivery methods. In spite of declining volumes, national operators in industrialised countries typically must deliver mail to residences and businesses 5 or 6 days each week. By contrast, delivery in Africa is done primarily through post office boxes

---

10 *Final Acts World Conference on Telecommunications, Dubai 2012*, available from: www.itu.int

11 The latter group was used to distribute government benefits, salaries, periodicals, literature, etc. and today can be characterised as having excess capacity (UPU, *Development of Postal Services in 2012*).

with only 6 national operators providing home delivery.[12] Furthermore, in much of the developing world, utility companies frequently self-deliver mail, using their own employees and address infrastructures.[13] Access to postal services of a standard quality is also a key universal service concept, as is the UPU-led drive to improve this quality to keep postal products competitive in an ever-faster communications market. However, low volumes, inadequate air connections and poor transportation and addressing infrastructures make it difficult for some national operators to meet the UPU's D+5 standard for international mail.[14]

IS UNIVERSAL SERVICE SUSTAINABLE?

Monopolies over mail carriage were first established centuries ago to ensure royal control over the distribution of information. As the concept of universal service grew, this was adopted to fit the economic concept that a network industry functioned most efficiently when a limited number of networks (ideally one) carried large volumes and achieved economies of scale. Outside the EU, many industrialised nations and most developing nations still grant at least a partial monopoly (usually a reserved area defined by weight, e.g. all letter-post items up to 350 grams) to the national operator. The efficacy of this mechanism in markets with low postal volumes has been challenged for some time.[15] Specifically it has been asserted that there is not enough mail in these markets (particularly where there is significant *de facto* market liberalisation due to low market-entry barriers) to support the provision of universal service.

---

12 Graeme Lee, 'Universal service in Africa', available from: www.PostalTechnologyInternational. com (accessed June 2012)

13 Ansón, José and Toledano, Joëlle, *Postal Economics in Developing Countries*, UPU, Bern, 2009

14 'D' = day of posting

15 Kenny, Charles, *Reforming the Posts: Abandoning the Monopoly-Supported Postal Universal Service Obligation in Developing Countries*, World Bank Policy Research Working Paper 3627, June 2005

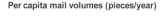

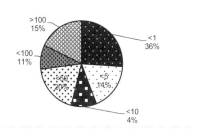

Figure 3: Per capita mail volumes (pieces/year) for national operators

As shown above, 54% of national operators reporting per capita mail volumes to the UPU have fewer than 10 pieces of mail per capita. In such scenarios, a monopoly, even if scrupulously observed, provides little support for universal service and makes it difficult to achieve economies of scale.[16] This is exacerbated in much of the developing world when basic postal *prices* are kept below costs for political reasons, despite the fact that 90–95% of mail volumes are generated by businesses and government rather than individuals. The impact of lower volumes and USO costs can be seen in the financial performance of national operators: for upper-income, higher-volume countries, approximately 25% have negative revenues; for lower- and middle-income countries, the number jumps to 50%.[17] If volumes continue to decline, at what point will a reserved area, no matter how comprehensive, cease to be a viable means for funding universal service? Some governments have initiated Universal Service Funds to support the USO, but most of these are in the developmental stage and it is not clear that they can generate sufficient resources to offset USO-related losses. At some future point, governments may be forced to ask whether postal services are commercial or a social necessity, and if the latter, how they rank with education, health, infrastructure and other critical areas in the allocation of scarce resources.

---

16   It could be argued that, since this data covers UPU operators, it does not represent the entire market. However, since it is the only mail used funding universal service, the analysis remains valid.

17   UPU, *Postal Statistics*

CAN UNIVERSAL POSTAL SERVICES SURVIVE IN A DIGITAL AGE?

It must be recognised that the current definition of universal services was developed in a pre-digital age. At the time, postal services were viewed as the most comprehensive and accessible form of communication, hence the concept that they should be universal. This is no longer the case and, *in sum, the right to communications no longer only means the right to postal services.* The postal sector must adapt to this new world, including its thinking regarding the nature of universal service.

The universal postal service definition must recognise the wider communications world that surrounds it as well as the need for the flexibility to respond to market forces and technological advances. As shown above, the definition of universality in the telecommunications sector reflects both demand and supply (access) by requiring *reasonable* access to service as opposed to access at *all points.* Furthermore, universality in the telecommunications sector has been further detailed by distinguishing *universal service* (US) – availability at the individual or household level through fixed lines and mobile devices – from *universal access* (UA) – availability through publicly shared cell phones, pay phones or Internet cafés.[18] In defining access 'gaps' in universal service, moreover, telecommunications policy differentiates between those that can be closed through increased market efficiency and those 'true gaps' requiring government intervention. Finally, due to rapid privatisation in the telecommunications sector, many governments distribute the USO among a number of operators. By contrast, in the postal sector the national operator is the sole operator required to fulfil the USO, even if it holds a minority share in the market and loses money by fulfilling the USO.

DEVELOPING A UNIVERSAL SERVICE FOR THE TWENTY-FIRST CENTURY: THE FUTURE IS NOW

Three key concepts have been addressed above:

1. Postal services are no longer the sole or the most accessible communications alternative

2. As postal volumes decline, there is increasing pressure on traditional

---

18 www.ictregulationtoolkit.org. In principle, universal service is only accessible when the user can pay for this service. In the postal sector, the user (except in the case of post-office boxes) does not pay for the service.

funding mechanisms (e.g. reserved areas) and on the national operators who must meet the USO

3. Current concepts and definitions of universal postal services do not adequately balance the mandated supply (accessibility) of these services with the existing demand for them.

How can these concepts help to shape a universal postal service that more accurately reflects the twenty-first-century communications market? Some suggestions include:

- *Develop a more comprehensive and inclusive universal service concept.* Postal services do not operate in a vacuum and should not depend on a stand-alone definition of their universality. Instead, this definition should be expanded into a larger vision of the services that are so essential that they must be universally available, including access to all communications and financial networks, government benefits, health and education facilities, etc. This 'basket' of universal services could be offered through the postal network or, alternatively, postal services could be offered through another essential service network.

- *Promote ICT–postal convergence.* Today, governments define one set of universal service standards and goals for digital communications and a separate one for postal services. If these are both communications services, it should be possible to develop a single, comprehensive universal communications network on a nationwide and international basis. The UPU and ITU are perfectly placed institutionally to develop a *universal communications concept* that would translate into greater ICT–postal convergence.

- *Adjust the USO to actual demand.* Universal service is currently defined in terms of access *at all points* to the supply of service. This can lead governments to extend service into underserved areas, without first determining whether demand for postal services exists. Instead, governments should consider a wide range of demand factors, including population, available power and transportation, level of commercial activity and so forth, when determining where to extend service. Furthermore, the growing value of postal services as transportation and logistics channels (e.g. parcels) should be highlighted along with their value as a communications network.

- *Consider narrowing the scope of the USO.* The Universal Postal Convention basically defines letter-post items as priority and non-priority items including letters, postcards, printed papers and small packets up to two kilograms; but does this represent the majority of mail being processed or customer needs? What would the impact be of lowering these limits to 1.0 kilograms or even less?

- *Consider guidance provided by the telecommunications policies.* The telecommunications sector has a policy framework that provides a more flexible approach to evaluating universal access and service. This framework may provide some alternatives to define universal postal services.

CONCLUSION

The irresistible forces reshaping the postal market will accelerate in the coming years and further challenge our traditional view of universal service and the postal industry itself. As we approach the 2016 UPU Congress in Turkey, it is certainly not too early to take up this fundamental issue. As a famous American football coach often said about planning for the future, 'The future is now!'[19]

QUESTION FOR THOUGHT AND DISCUSSION

What should happen to the Universal Service Obligation – is it still relevant and, if so, what form should it take and how should it be defined? If convergence of the postal and ICT sectors is happening, what are the opportunities or imperatives for the UPU and ITU to collaborate more closely?

---

19 Motto of George Allen, American football coach, active 1948–1990 (see www.wikepedia.org)

SECTION 6
CHANGING PERSPECTIVES AND PERCEPTIONS

Edited by Graeme Lee

Sunflower Associates

This section builds on the questions asked in the final article of the previous section. The World is changing but is the postal sector changing at the same speed? According to Cisco, the number of mobile devices and connections has grown to seven billion, virtually one for every human being on earth. Smartphones alone have grown in number by almost half a billion, with each smartphone generating 29 times more traffic than a non-smart device. One only has to walk the streets of any country in the world to see that the humble mobile phone is a ubiquitous accessory. From schoolchildren in Africa to lunching ladies in London, the mobile phone is a necessity, a truly universal system of communication.

But what are posts doing to embrace ICT? In their future strategies, posts can adopt approaches that focus on the purely physical, which would include postal and logistics services. Or they can adopt more ICT-focused services that allow them to utilise post-office networks for retail and banking services. A third approach is to focus on an ICT strategy that links the virtual and physical worlds by providing a one-stop shop for financial, retail, postal and logistics services through a postal portal. It is interesting that the traditionally powerful posts of Europe and North America are more focused on the physical strategy, albeit with significant investment in ICT, while several posts in Asia are focused on ICT services through their retail outlets.

In this section, three authors from diverse backgrounds question the impact ICT will have on the sector and how posts must engage with ICT to secure their future.

Hans Kok opens the section by questioning the relevance of universal postal service in Africa in light of ICT developments. He shows how posts have a universal service that is met in only a few countries. By contrast, telecoms do not have universal service commitments, yet many countries have achieved over 100% mobile penetration. He follows Juan Ianni's call for more coordinated ICT policies that include the postal sector. While his article is focused on the situation in Africa, the questions raised are just as relevant for the rest of the world.

Ian Streule follows with an article questioning the future of posts providing communication and financial services, given recent developments in ICT. Ian focuses on two possible futures and the organisational requirements for each. What is interesting about Ian's article is that it paints both a bleak and a bright future for posts irrespective of the future path taken. A bright future will require significant change and for postal companies to embrace the possibilities enabled by ICT developments.

Gareth Locksley postulates that posts will be 'the same, only different' in the digital economy. The digital economy will generate new demand for services leading to an increased requirement for delivery of packets and parcels. This is good news for the postal sector but may not be good news for national postal operators. National operators will face more competition in these open markets and will need to learn the language of the digital economy in order to compete.

Do new developments sound the death knell for national postal operators or do they offer them a chance to reinvent themselves?

WHAT IS THE RELEVANCE OF UNIVERSAL POSTAL SERVICE IN AFRICA IN LIGHT OF ICT DEVELOPMENTS?

Hans Kok

Business Consult, The Netherlands

INTRODUCTION

In postal-sector reform, much of the focus is on European and Asia-Pacific countries where national postal operators are involved in major transformation processes over a number of years. These developments provide many learning opportunities for those operators still facing deeper postal reforms, as is the case in Africa.

What about Africa? What can be expected in Africa for the national postal sector of each country? Do new developments sound the death knell for national postal operators or do they offer them a chance to reinvent themselves? And what will happen to universal service provision, which was the rationale to grant Designated Postal Operators (DPOs) the obligation to provide basic postal services nationwide? Is the universal service obligation a curse or an opportunity and what are the conditions to succeed? This article provides some views based on my own experiences over many years working with postal institutions in Africa.

AFRICA OVERVIEW

Africa has 55 countries and there is a huge differentiation between them in respect to economic development, population, geography, area and culture. When analysing Africa it is also interesting to make comparisons with Europe, especially being involved myself in postal reforms in many EU countries (PHARE program) and within the EU as a whole in the period 1970–2012[1]. I have also worked on postal projects in many African countries since 1995 and in a recent postal-sector reform study on behalf of the African Union (AU) in 2012[2]. The table below compares some of the key issues facing the European and African Unions.

European Union	African Union
EU: initially 12, later 15 and now 27 countries	AU: 54 countries, also segmented in Regional Economic Communities (RECs) with own policies
Serious differences in development between countries but state institutions more or less functioning in general	Huge differences in development between countries with many countries having no, or hardly functioning, state institutions
Aiming at establishing an internal market and full market liberalisation; promoting postal-sector reforms to encourage country policy makers to move in a market-oriented direction	Aiming at harmonisation of policies and not yet the establishment of an internal market; no serious interest in the postal sector or with setting direction for policy makers
Nationwide coverage of public services (water, electricity, roads, telephone and post) generally realised; customers looking for value-added services	Nationwide covering of public services limited by socio-economic conditions and far from providing universal provision

It is also useful to compare postal-sector reforms in the two unions:

European postal sector	African postal sector
Most countries over 100, and up to 400, mail items per capita per annum	Most countries below 1 mail item per capita per annum, only a few have 10–20 per capita
Post increasingly seen as normal enterprise with some additional public functions, while market-orientation guarantees the future	Post still predominantly part of state institutions, with posts still too dependent on government policies
Universal postal service has impact for nationwide coverage and access, while all other (value-added) services are not regulated	Universal postal service remains a higher objective with ongoing serious limitations in coverage and access
Cost-based postal services enable increasingly balancing the books or making profits to invest in diversification	Cost allocation in many countries below standards, making proper management impossible and also limiting investments in new value-added services

1   ECORYS reports: Development of competition in the postal sector 2004–2005 and Main developments in the postal sector 2006–2008 on behalf of the European Commission in Brussels

2   Report on Consultancy services on elaboration of a model and guidelines on Universal Postal Service (UPS) for Africa, on behalf of African Union in Addis Ababa, January 2013 (with Graeme Lee)

European postal sector	African postal sector
Near to cost-covering or profitable national postal operators	Mostly loss-making national postal operators reliant on government subsidies
From 1989 Green Paper, followed by EU Directives aiming at market liberalisation, realised in January 2012	Still in initial phase of harmonisation of policies without a clear perspective for where this will lead

In Europe, there were differences between markets in best- and worst-case scenarios, but all countries had a functioning, and universal, postal service. In Africa, the differences are incomparable with worst-case scenarios having no functioning post offices and the best cases providing daily delivery to every home. It is therefore important in Africa to address the needs of the postal sector on a country by country basis.

FUTURE UNIVERSAL POSTAL SERVICES IN AFRICA

Of course there are many more differences that could be mentioned but for the moment the aspects above enable us to draw relevant conclusions for what is important for the future of a universal postal service (UPS) in Africa:

1. For UPS, the general UPU definition[3] is still useful in Africa in defining the minimum expectations of a national postal operator. But the devil is in the detail, and the question is how it is elaborated in postal laws and regulations in terms of access and quality of service standards for the whole country.

2. UPS is a general (higher) objective in national development policies and postal sector policies but in most countries it has very limited impact and there is insufficient coverage and access. Increasing access and improving quality of service provision are still key to development.

3. UPS coverage and access objectives in many countries are not elaborated in concrete measureable targets, preventing evaluation of their progress by the policy maker and postal regulator. Regulatory authorities still have a long way to go to enforce effective postal regulations in many African countries.

4. UPS in Africa is still predominantly provided through PO Boxes, which have serious limitations in offering real quality of service.

5. UPS is focused on how to reach rural communities, while Africa is

---

3   UPU Congress in Beijing 1999 and Bucharest 2004 standard definitions

experiencing massive urbanisation[4]. If more focus were given to connecting the new urbanites, the objective of providing more people with access to postal and other public services might be more easily realised.

6. UPS is aimed at providing basic mail services, while many designated postal operators in Africa already have a dominant revenue base from value-added CEP[5] and logistical services, (postal) financial services, agency services and/or retail services. Too many countries do not enable the post to participate in diversification of services and development of financial services.

7. Within UPS, smaller operators (and private messengers) have become active, especially passenger transport (bus) companies, which are often not subject to postal regulations[6] and which provide service along popular routes and offer value-added services (speed, same-day, secured delivery with signatures).

8. Designated postal operators have a UPS obligation to provide services for small packets and parcels despite this area being part of the competitive CEP market dominated by private-sector operators with no nationwide obligations.

9. Mobile communications and Internet access in Africa are increasingly providing what the post never has: access for all.

Outside the core postal markets, the volumes and development for value-added services show healthy growth (courier and express, logistics, retail and financial services etc.). At the same time, ordinary mail in all countries is under threat of substitution by electronic media and postal operators not able to diversify will struggle to remain viable. Diversification of value-added services is dependent on ICT development. ICT is fundamental for support services, management information and costing systems, and is essential for provision of track and trace, counter automation, Internet-based solutions and remote delivery options.

---

4   Not only are there more people living in cities but the cities themselves are becoming larger and more numerous. There are now 43 cities in Africa with populations of more than one million inhabitants, a figure which is expected to increase to almost 70 by 2015 (UN reports on urbanisation in Africa).

5   Courier Express and Parcels market (CEP)

6   Even more tragic are those cases where postal operators lack transport means and have to use local bus companies.

PERSPECTIVE FOR MORE ICT-BASED POSTAL-SECTOR POLICIES

The main question is where such development comes from, as most national postal operators are state owned, state funded and, in many countries, still managed as state enterprises.

Where posts are corporatised the situation is better, but the state is still the main entity responsible for creating an enabling environment for ICT-based postal services. Hereafter, I will try to indicate some principle efforts that need to be made in postal policy and restructuring.

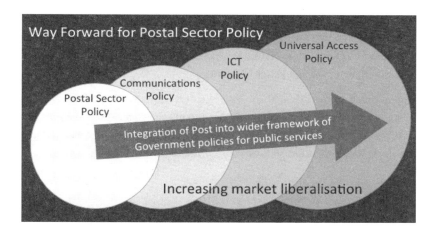

The picture above indicates four phases of postal policy development, which may take place in distinct phases or show parallel developments in two or more areas.

a. Development of a **Postal Sector Policy** has taken place since 2000[7] but is still not finalised or implemented in most countries. While such policies clearly define the roles for policy maker, regulator and universal service providers, they usually fail to make clear expectations for coverage and access. Service in urban areas should be improved, while ensuring reasonable service in rural areas: designated operators should be enabled to diversify their business through investment or partnership; designated operators should build their business strategies on ICT development.

---

7 Examples: South Africa White Paper 1998, Zimbabwe 2001, Tanzania 2003, Mozambique 2008, Namibia 2009

b. Develop a **Communications Policy** with post viewed as a key part of the communications sector where facilities are used for a range of related services. To date, development of such policies has focused on telecommunications, leaving the post isolated.

c. Develop an **ICT Policy**, which has become fashionable[8] over the last few years, covering the communications sector as a whole (telecommunications, ICT, post and broadcasting) and enabling a better service provision and increased access for all sectors.

d. **Universal Access policies**, which incorporate telecommunication, ICT and postal policy with regards to improving coverage and access to the rural population for all services. However, some recently drafted policies[9] make the mistake of excluding the post. A positive example is the recently drafted (January 2014) National Integrated ICT Policy Green Paper in South Africa[10], which does include the post.

It has to be taken into account that new policies take place in a de facto and de jure liberalising market environment where partnerships are necessary to combine huge investments in infrastructure and ICT-based services. If the post gets isolated in this development, the future will be more difficult and in the end universal postal services will suffer.

CONCLUSION

In response to the questions posed at the start of my article, I have reached the following conclusions:

A. What is to be expected in Africa for the national postal sector of each country? Do new developments sound the death knell for national postal operators or do they offer them a chance to reinvent themselves?

It is clear that in failed states[11] there is nothing to be expected from the national postal operator. But in many countries, designated postal operators are reinventing themselves as the main provider for postal financial services, which are already the main source of revenues for several. Many

---

8   Examples: North Africa Algeria and Tunisia since 2001; South Africa Green Paper 2014

9   Examples: Recently drafted policies in Botswana 2011 and Zambia 2013

10   South Africa Government Gazette/Staatskoerant Vol. 583, 24 January 2014, National Integrated ICT Policy Green Paper

11   Examples: Central African Republic and Congo Democratic Republic

DPOs[12] have succeeded in getting a significant part of the market in value-added services as well, while others see no credibility in being a player in such markets. Success factors include having a strong postal-sector policy, a clear legal and regulatory framework providing reasonable targets for quality of service for basic (universal) postal services and, last but not least, adequate governance instruments and control mechanisms[13] to establish an active and accountable national postal operator. In all these areas, there is still a lot of work to be done.

B. What will happen to universal service provision, which was the rationale to grant Designated Postal Operators (DPOs) the obligation to provide basic postal services nationwide? Is the universal service obligation a curse or an opportunity and what are the conditions of success?

In my view the universal service provision is still important for the DPO as most have a positive balance of terminal dues from incoming cross-border mail for delivery in the most densely populated areas. Modernisation of postal services in urban and industrial areas and capturing market volumes through diversified services in these areas will enable DPOs to maintain a basic level of universal postal services.

Having the most extensive network for services in many countries is still an opportunity, provided DPOs manage to modernise their post offices into effective and efficient service points and enter partnerships to develop new postal services.

Success factors include: a more independent national postal operator with adequate funding to invest in upgraded basic postal services; revised strategies and business re-design enabling public–private partnerships in better and new service provision; revamping management practices and human-resource policies.

While the physical transfer of messages will continue to be overtaken by the electronic transfer of messages, it is essential that posts diversify into value-added services and enhance existing products and services. Modern ordinary mail solutions, PO Box developments, hybrid mail solutions, courier and express, logistics, financial services and e-government services are all products that can be offered using a modern ICT platform.

---

12 Examples: South Africa, Botswana, Namibia, Morocco and Algeria
13 Incorporation of DPO, performance contracts, annual reporting, proper cost accounting, etc.

Posts should be fully enabled to participate in ICT developments as part of wider universal access policies. It is essential that governments no longer view communications as disparate sectors but instead provide a converged regulatory environment that allows the whole sector to prosper together. Post offices in Africa provide an opportunity to provide access for ICT, financial services, government services and physical delivery in rural areas but only if they are included as part of a wider access policy.

QUESTION FOR THOUGHT AND DISCUSSION

Are there some common 'prescriptions' for African postal operators and, if so, how should they be taken forward, given that most posts are still bound up with their governments? How much can individual postal companies take control of their future themselves and drive their own destiny based on their particular needs?

...the opportunities for ICT in providing communication and financial services are extremely promising, whereas the prospects for conventional physical postal services are mixed.

WHAT IS THE FUTURE OF POSTS GIVEN RECENT DEVELOPMENTS OF ICT IN PROVIDING COMMUNICATION AND FINANCIAL SERVICES?

Ian Streule

Analysys Mason Limited

INTRODUCTION

The short answer to this question is that there is more than one possible future for posts: which one occurs will depend on the states of communication services and economic development in the country in question. Here I will set out two possible futures for the postal industry. It is up to the business leaders of individual companies to decide which future they seek to achieve – both are possible, but the organisational requirements for each are dramatically different.

The background to these future scenarios is the same – that the opportunities for ICT in providing communication and financial services are extremely promising, whereas the prospects for conventional physical postal services are mixed.

THE RATE OF GROWTH IN ICT SECTORS

The last ten years have been characterised by enormous ICT growth, especially in mobile communications technologies. This growth has had a direct impact on depressing the demand for traditional postal and associated GPO services, and this is expected to persist.

The evolution of ICT may be illustrated by two recent trends: smartphones and mobile money. Figure 1[1] presents the worldwide penetration of mobile-phone handsets (of all types), smartphones and 4G handsets. It can be seen that, although handset penetration is already high (more than 80% in 2013 and expected to reach 100% by 2018), the penetration of smartphones is growing quickly (standing at around 20% in 2013 but expected to reach around 50% by 2018).

Smartphones are a key enabler for a broad base of communication possibilities and varied private, social and business-to-business ICT applications. Government agencies already recognise the effectiveness of Internet and advanced mobile communications to deliver e-government services.

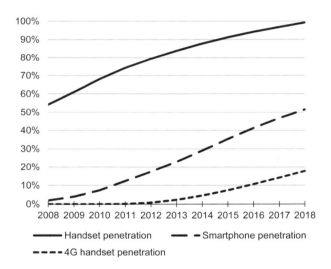

Figure 1: Worldwide penetration of handsets, smartphones and 4G handsets
Source: Analysys Mason, 2014

Figure 2 presents the use of mobile money services (mobile money transfer services) in three large developing markets – South Africa, Nigeria and Kenya.

These innovative services were initially popular in some developing nations, but

1   Figures 1 to 3 are taken from Analysys Mason, *Global telecoms market: interim forecast update 2013–2018*, available from: http://www.analysysmason.com/Templates/Pages/KnowledgeCentreArticle1.aspx?id=14028

are now being launched and adopted in other regions of the world, including in developed Europe and Asia. The availability of monetary currency on a mobile phone or smartphone increases the opportunities for seamless, paperless commerce, and access to banking and e-shopping anywhere.

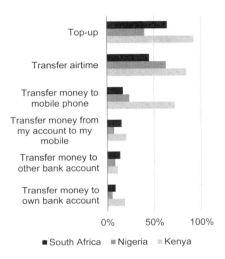

Figure 2: Reported use of mobile money transfer services in South Africa, Nigeria and Kenya
Source: Analysys Mason, 2014[2]

THE RATE OF CHANGE IN THE POSTAL INDUSTRY

When we contrast these fast-growing ICT services with the postal industry, we see a mixed picture. This is illustrated in Figure 3.

Connectivity to modern electronic communications networks is increasing strongly. Globally, only fixed voice connections are in decline, but this is more than outweighed by the growth in fixed broadband and mobile voice connectivity. Turning to the postal sector, traditional letter items are expected to decline significantly over the next five years. However, the outlook for packets and parcels is promising, with steady growth predicted.

---

2   Respondents were 2,250 mobile Internet users in South Africa, Nigeria and Kenya. They were asked the question 'Which of the following have you done using your mobile phone?'

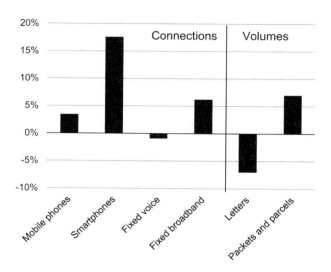

Figure 3: Annual growth rates in communications expected over the next five years, global estimates

Source: Analysys Mason, 2014

IN THE FUTURE, WILL IT BE ECONOMIES OF SCALE OR ECONOMIES OF SCOPE?

Today, information and communications technologies are evolving much faster than postal services. ICTs can be reconfigured electronically on a rapid basis to meet the needs of established and new users. Over-the-top (OTT) services can emerge even without any change to the ICT infrastructure, as the development focuses on the 'application layer'.

On the other hand, physical conveyance networks designed to carry tangible items cannot be reconfigured electronically: they must be restructured physically. Additional 'applications' can be offered within physical conveyance networks, leveraging the physical infrastructure and points of presence – for example, financial services. However, these additional applications often have a physical embodiment such as the presence of the customer in the retail premises, or rely on the trusted relationship between the customer and the postal provider.

ICT can be employed within the network, for optimising business operations, tracking items and offering e-services to customers, but fundamentally the postal industry is still a physical network.

I see two different strategies for the postal industry – to seek out growth and profitability either from *economies of scale* or from *economies of scope*, as illustrated in Figure 4.

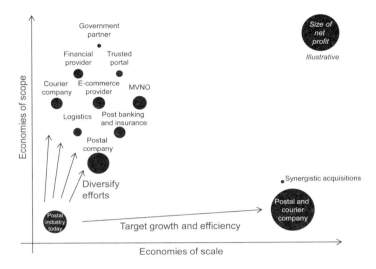

Figure 4: Future strategies for the postal industry

Source: Analysys Mason, 2014

STRATEGY 1: SEEK ECONOMIES OF SCOPE BY DIVERSIFYING EFFORTS

The postal industry sits adjacent to many other segments of commercial and social activity, as shown in Figure 4. Diversification and cross-selling strategies aim at these segments. This approach can be particularly geared towards broadening the role of national postal incumbents, as they are likely to have a strong brand, trusted customer relationships and a nationwide network.

In developed countries, this strategy will inevitably involve following the ICT revolution with a 'me-too' postal-branded alternative. At first sight, that does not appear to be a very attractive proposition, but it depends on the local environment for multi-sector companies. In some developing countries, where the level of ICT development is lower and approaching a likely expansion phase, the postal industry has the opportunity successfully to lead this growth, potentially using strong government support for the (former) state-owned incumbent to be the provider of choice.

Building a broad portfolio of consumer and business services should aim to provide an end-to-end customer experience, from ordering, paying, processing through to receiving the final goods and services on offer. Options for physical or electronic communication should be offered seamlessly to users.

For success, consumers and businesses ideally should choose: post e-mail *not* g-mail; post bank *not* commercial bank; e-commerce where the postal company is there to satisfy the need for end-to-end reliability *not* whoever might be cheapest on the day; post mobile (MVNO) *not* multinational telecoms operator; the trusted national postal industry *not* transient or international service suppliers.

Needs: For this outcome, the postal industry must invest in adjacent sectors, move fast and build on its brands. This needs dynamic management with insight and entrepreneurial spirit. Importantly, this approach aims to meet the diverse needs of the market and the complexity of this cannot be underestimated. Furthermore, it is also expected that not all ventures will succeed – this strategy has risks, but some ventures may pay off. There are examples of successful post banks, postal MVNOs, ancillary services and so forth.

Poste Mobile is the largest virtual mobile network operator in Italy, in the market since late 2007 and currently with about 3 million active customers. Poste Mobile makes use of the commercial network of 14,000 post offices.

The key to the success of Poste Mobile has been the ability to enter the competitive telecoms market with an offering that combines the convenience of mobile communication services with traditional voice, data and texting, plus an innovative range of financial services, information and devices, m-payments, m-banking and m-commerce. These are accessible through the association of the Poste Mobile SIM card with the Banco Posta means of payment (current account or card).

These services are accessible through the menu of the SIM on the mobile phone or through Poste Mobile apps downloaded on smartphones.[3]

The trick here is to join all these elements together and achieve the economies of scope of a multi-faceted, future-oriented company offering financial, information and communications services.

---

3   Summarised from: http://www.postemobile.it/chi-siamo/la-societa

STRATEGY 2: SEEK ECONOMIES OF SCALE BY TARGETING GROWTH AND EFFICIENCY

Despite all the seemingly or realistically attractive adjacent segments, this strategy takes the opposite approach. It aims to leave the emerging electronic communications, ICT and financial services to the modern ICT providers: mobile operators, Internet providers, commercial banks, business service providers and agile fast-moving entrepreneurs.

The postal industry is labour intensive, and requires extensive physical and mechanical handling activities to deliver its core services. The organisational skills to run the postal industry are a long way from the management requirements of the future ICT industry. This strategy recognises the fundamental reductions expected to be seen in letter volumes, but seeks to maximise the sector's involvement in growth areas where they do exist.

Core business activities may require interconnection and work-sharing where there are more efficient arrangements to be found. However, the purpose is to carry as many items as possible, and profitably. New technologies and innovations can be found to support this growth and the variety is large: flexible delivery points, real-time track-and-trace, precision delivery timing, flexible returns and rerouting options, innovation in service pricing, e-commerce partnerships and so forth.

Needs: To achieve economies of scale, the postal industry must optimise its cost structure and support the maximum possible volume of items. This requires management with a strong focus on the core logistics, sorting and delivery activities – the functions of a single-minded postal industry. Small synergistic businesses could be acquired to support niche aspects of the overall strategy. However, this approach is not without downsides – as letter volumes decline, the industry is likely to face declining revenues and probably lower staff numbers. Nevertheless, there is evidence of successful postal companies demonstrating their singular objectives to be the best physical networks

Royal Mail in the UK is promoting its trust amongst consumers as the parcel-delivery partner for online retailers: 'We love parcels. In fact, we deliver 1 billion of them a year. We're launching our new Christmas TV advert, the first in six years, featuring our postmen and women, showing what they do best: delivering parcels to people across the nation'[4].

---

4   http://www.royalmailgroup.com/royal-mail-launches-tv-campaign-targeting-businesses

The challenge is a concentrated management and workforce effort on optimisation, innovation and cost efficiency, combined with the best possible support for growth areas – higher profits may then be achieved, to the benefit of continued innovation and investment.

CONCLUSION

The communications and ICT industry continues to grow strongly and serves a wide range of personal, social, financial, business and governmental needs. The future of posts in this context is twofold. I see the possibility for the postal industry to diversify and engage in a wide variety of adjacent, market-oriented segments; or conversely, to focus and optimise on physical logistics, conveyance and delivery. Both approaches have opportunities for sustainable profitability, but different risks in achieving the outcome. The decision as to which strategic direction to take remains with the management boards, and will definitely vary for each country and stage of economic and technological development.

QUESTION FOR THOUGHT AND DISCUSSION

Either of the two main strategies outlined here, scope or scale, would provide a possible future direction for a post; but which direction is best for your organisation and what are the advantages or disadvantages of each? Must it be one or the other?

Postal services were important in agrarian economies, developed in industrial economies and adapted significantly in service economies, a trajectory that is likely to be followed in the digital economy.

THE SAME, ONLY DIFFERENT: POSTAL SERVICES IN THE DIGITAL ECONOMY

Gareth Locksley
Sunflower Associates

INTRODUCTION

In March 2014, the Internet reached its 25th birthday and for many of us, life without it is unimaginable. Now access to superfast broadband with data rates over 100 mbps, frequently using wireless technologies, is commonplace. In this same period, ICT devices have become ubiquitous, with many of them communicating automatically with each other rather than us to form the 'Internet of Things'. Together ICT devices and broadband networks are the foundations of the digital economy. What does this development mean for postal services?

Economies continuously undergo developments of varying intensity and focus. We have experienced agrarian, industrial and service economies and are now entering the Internet-enabled or digital economy. The industrial economy did not displace the agrarian economy; rather, the methods and products of industry were applied to agriculture. Now the weight of agriculture in the overall economy is low but agricultural output has never been higher. True, some activities appear to become extinct, but actually they remain by adapting to economic and technological evolution.

Postal services were important in agrarian economies, developed in industrial economies and adapted significantly in service economies, a trajectory that is likely to be followed in the digital economy. The widespread adoption of always-on fixed and mobile broadband, then superfast broadband, smart ICT devices and their application to an ever-increasing range of activities is very likely to mean that in future the role of postal services will be the same, only different and probably bigger. That is, if postal services embed broadband into all aspects of their businesses; if not, the role will be the same but considerably smaller.

Postal services are experienced platform providers (see below) in an open ICT ecosystem that increasingly favours platforms. The digital economy will generate more parcels, more opportunities for collaboration in technology, finance and as resellers; all to the potential advantage of postal services. But in this open ecosystem, failure to embrace the potential advantages of ICT will seriously restrict the business of existing postal services.

ICT ECOSYSTEM

The ICT sector can be considered as a form of 'ecosystem'[1] characterised by significant interaction between the various ICT players. The nature and evolution of this ecosystem has important ramifications for efficiency, innovation and competitiveness. There are three layers in the ecosystem plus customers. These layers are:

1. Network element suppliers (e.g. Cisco, Samsung, Alcatel, Huawei, Intel)

2. Network operators (fixed and mobile) (e.g. Verizon, Orange, Telefonica, China Telecom)

3. Platform, content, application providers (e.g. Google, i-store, YouTube, Alibaba).

For many years, the dominant set of interactions was between layers 1 and 2, giving rise to innovation processes that tended to exclude other players and tended to keep profits among network suppliers and operators (i.e. this was a 'closed' ecosystem). But with widespread and affordable access to the Internet, the ecosystem began to evolve. In the broadband era, the ecosystem is evolving at an accelerating rate which will quicken in the superfast broadband era.

Increasingly, competition and cooperation in the ecosystem takes place between and within platforms. A platform is an open system with well-defined enforceable rules and access points on which third parties can build applications (apps) or offer services or provide content. In this way, Layer 3 becomes a focus for, and key

---

1   See, for example: Veugeller, R., 'New ICT Sectors: platforms for European growth?', Bruegal Policy Contribution, August 2012

enabler of, innovation. The key to this process is widespread and affordable access to broadband for those who want to buy/experience and those that want to sell/create.

Now ecosystem interactions are much more inclusive and 'open' so that there are many more players and profits are more widely spread. One aspect of this evolution is the mass of (non-traditional) user-generated content on broadband networks. Another is the generalised fracturing of boundaries between layers, the sheer volume of new entrants and the much enhanced role of Layer 3.

Layer 3 players are driving changes in the ecosystem and the innovation process through their interaction with each other and final customers/users. Layer 3 players interact digitally as intermediaries with businesses that want to sell and businesses/consumers that want to buy, or people who wish to create and audiences who wish to experience. This intermediation takes place on a global scale over broadband infrastructure and covers both material and non-material goods and services. Such intermediation in such volumes and of such complexity is a new paradigm.

All of this will be very familiar to the providers of postal services with their extensive expertise as platform providers operating on a global scale with correspondents and material goods and services. There is even an analogue for user-generated content, for example individuals, non-traditional traders and new parcel senders. The challenge for the postal sector is to innovate by applying the ever-evolving ICT and broadband to their internal modus operandi (efficiency and productivity) as well as to their role in intermediation in the knowledge that, if they do not step up (competitiveness), somebody else will, since the ecosystem is open.

TOWARDS THE DIGITAL ECONOMY

In an era of low growth and austerity, most governments have identified the benefits of broadband[2] (now recognised as a general-purpose technology) and have implemented policies to promote investment and access thereby driving the Internet-enabled digital economy. For instance, the EU's policy-oriented 'Digital Agenda for Europe' established a scoreboard with 13 broad targets for 2015, five of which are particularly pertinent to postal services:

+ 33% of SME selling online

+ 20% of population buying online cross border

---

2   See, for example: European Commission, 'The socio-economic benefits of bandwidth', 2013

- 50% of population buying online

- 50% of population using e-government

- 25% of population using e-government and returning forms.

Digital technologies lower the costs of doing business in two ways[3]. Firstly, they reduce the costs of selling goods by lowering the cost of distributing products and collecting payments, known as transaction costs. The cost advantages of online stores over their bricks-and-mortar competitors are that they can offer more variety, manage assortments, communicate choices and prices to consumers more easily and do not face space constraints. Secondly, the technologies lower the costs of buying goods, known as search costs. Buyers can use search and recommendation engines together with one-click options to reduce significantly the effort of finding products that match their tastes and price points. Major retailers (from groceries to electronics) are pushing online sales (locally and globally) so, while the number of forms and flyers in physical transit may fall, the population of packages is on the rise. All this translates as 'more parcels, but different'.

According to the Ecommerce Europe's B2C Report 2013[4] there were 250 million e-shoppers in Europe, each on average spending €1,243 with those in the UK spending €96 billion, €50 billion in Germany and €45 billion in France. The organisation estimates that these activities accounted for 3.5 billion B2C parcels within Europe. B2B e-commerce is also growing[5] along with e-procurement and e-invoicing. Alibaba of China is one of the very biggest Internet-based traders with $150 billion worth of merchandise changing hands on its platforms per year, more than Amazon.com and eBay combined. Successfully addressing this market is vital for the postal services.

The App Economy started with the launch of the Apple App Store in 2008 and now there are more than 1 million apps available, generating well over 100 billion downloads. Recent estimates[6] of the contribution of the App Economy in the EU include 794,000 jobs across the whole economy, 529,000 direct App Economy jobs, 60% of which are developers. Twenty-two per cent of the global production of app-related products and services comes from the EU, with revenues of more than €10 billion per annum.

---

3   See Elberse, Anita (2014) 'Blockbusters', London: Faber & Faber

4   http://www.ecommerce-europe.eu/facts-figures

5   For the UK in 2008 estimated at GBP 360 billion by Office of National Statistics

6   http://www.visionmobile.com/product/the-european-app-economy/

Taking these and other factors into consideration, the Boston Consultancy Group (BCG) quantified the impact of the Internet (and Internet-enabled activities) on individual economies by assessing its contribution to GDP[7]. For 2010, BCG found the average contribution of the Internet for G-20 countries was 4.3% of GDP, with a range from 1.3% in Indonesia to 8.3% for the UK, with the average for the EU standing at 3.8% of GDP and growing. This is already bigger than the contribution of agriculture and it cannot be ignored by the postal sector.

ICT ENABLED ADVANTAGES

BCG also found that, for intensive web-user SMEs, the rates of sales growth were 22% higher (over a three-year period) than those of low- or non-web-user SMEs. In the UK, intensive-web-use SMEs grew sales six times faster than those with no Internet presence. There is also evidence that high-web-user companies have an international customer base and tend to generate more new jobs.

Postal services have to adopt the technology to make attractive propositions to these prospective clients. But SMEs have an advantage in embracing the technology because they are not burdened by large legacy assets, a factor which may challenge the postal sector.

For companies, the 'Internet advantage' is derived from a combination of the following factors:

- Geographic expansion – a wider customer base, sometimes without a physical presence

- Enhanced marketing and profitable sales from 'long-tail' products to sub-markets

- Improved interactions with customers, suppliers and partners

- Leveraging the Cloud by accessing sophisticated tools

- Improved automation and information exchange

- Easier and quicker staff recruitment.

Each factor has a potential to enhance efficiency or productivity which, when realised, strengthens competitiveness. Clearly, once the technology has been fully adopted, these advantages are available in postal services and should inform

---

7   See 'The Connected Kingdom: how the internet is transforming the UK economy', 2010 and 'The Internet Economy in the G-20', 2012 both BCG Connected World

business strategies regarding understanding and addressing customers, suppliers, partners and competitors. Many technology developments and apps are logistics-related and utilise the Cloud, 'the Internet of Things', GIS mapping, smart grids, smart meters, location technology, big-data analytics, digital modelling, simulation and visualisation, social and collaborative technologies, just-in-time supply, traffic-flow management, IT-enabled supply chains and so forth, all with relevance to postal services. Moreover, broadband and superfast broadband multiply these advantages.

THE COLLABORATIVE ECONOMY

Postal services have been founded on the principle of collaborative intermediation. Collaboration, using ICT advantages, is a key to success in the open digital ecosystem. Clearly there will be cooperation with other similar platforms outside domestic markets as well as inside, where postal services are a key input to a trader. Further, the sector will want to ensure that their technology needs for networks, hardware and apps are given the required degree of responsiveness from layers 1, 2 and 3. But there may be a strong business case for the creation of strong partnerships with network providers and other enablers of the digital economy.

Postal services have strong brands, extensive customer-facing networks, detailed local knowledge and big data. These characteristics could be very attractive to a broadband network operator (fixed or mobile) seeking a partner to resell its services. Such a partnership would provide the postal sector with immediate access to a new generation of customers for traditional and new e-based services. In a similar manner one of the key enablers of the digital economy is platforms that provide trust, security and encryption which would benefit from the characteristics of postal services in a reselling partnership. Furthermore any postal or logistics enterprise must work closely with such security enablers to protect their businesses from cybercrime.

Outside the 'free' digital economy, some form of electronic payments system is required. A recent report by the US Inspector General for Postal Services[8] estimated there were 68 million US citizens 'on the fringes of the banking system' and thereby not full participants in the digital economy. The purchase of reloadable, prepaid cards would facilitate participation and where better to obtain them than the customer-facing postal network working in partnership with sound financial institutions?

---

8   https://www.uspsoig.gov/sites/default/files/document-library-files/2014/rarc-wp-14-007.pdf

New entrants, often start-ups, are constantly providing new apps. These technology suppliers will be looking to partner with other platform providers like postal services because of the above characteristics and as a possible source of finance. This opportunity requires the sectors to apply their Internet advantage to assess (even incubate) these opportunities in the light of their knowledge of existing and potential customers as well as diversification strategies in an open ecosystem.

CONCLUSION

The general public, governments, entrepreneurs and social organisations are embracing the ICT and the digital economy. While ecosystems, products, services and methods are being transformed in the online world, there will be even more parcels to be paid for, tracked and shipped, and more potential partners in search of access to the valuable characteristics of postal services. There will also be more competition because there are more opportunities. But postal services possess advantages which, if successfully exploited internally as well as in facing existing and new customers, should see the post as a key platform of the digital economy.

As we enter the digital economy, what will be the future for postal services – the same only different!

QUESTION FOR THOUGHT AND DISCUSSION

The different layers of the ICT ecosystem are clearly explained here, along with the many opportunities to collaborate on these platforms. Does the post have to be a 'platform in the digital system' or is there an equivalent physical ecosystem in which posts can play a leading role? Can the posts play the 'same, but different' role in both the digital and physical ecosystems? Are they different systems or is there some strategic space where they overlap?

SECTION 7
CHANGING THE FUTURE FOR POSTS

Derek Osborn

In one sense, changing the future for posts is what this whole book is about. However, this section deals with some of the specific choices facing the postal industry and businesses within it. The sector is being redefined and the post is being reinvented continually in many places and ways – and with different results.

What are the opportunities available when reviewing the postal landscape and what are some of the main considerations for posts to consider when planning for the future? It is often said that 'the best way to predict the future is to create it'. So what kind of future can the posts begin to create?

Elmar Toime poses the strategic choice, as he sees it, between logistics and financial services which, he explains, are two very different kinds of business. In fact, their current integration within a postal company is largely because of their historical connection. He argues that the choice available is about business purpose – what is a postal company for? If posts follow the logic of this argument then the future for logistics may be quite different to that for postal counter or financial services.

João Melo starts by identifying the major societal changes currently taking place which are leading to new lifestyles but also to new business opportunities for posts. The key challenge, he maintains, is for posts to respond to this changing world and see what opportunities it affords for the provision of services that meet new customer requirements and expectations.

Olaf Klargaard and **Philippe Régnard** take this idea further by exploring how posts can build digital solutions on their trusted brand. The whole question of the extent to which posts engage in the digital arena is clearly pivotal to future options and it is maintained here that there are definitely opportunities for posts if they focus on their structural advantages and integrate digital services with their core physical assets. They then discuss an open model and integrated ecosystem as being key to providing new services and applications for consumers and broadening reach into new markets.

The 'open model' theme is continued by **Bernhard Bukovc**, who advocates an open innovation platform for the sector. No post needs to face the future alone and he sets out the advantages, but also the difficulties, of proceeding with a multilateral approach. Clearly there are real benefits from sharing experiences and knowledge, as well as collaborating in many different ways, in order to secure a better future for all players in the postal industry.

This book is intended to be a small contribution to this kind of wide-ranging and collaborative open platform for discussion, understanding, sharing ideas and innovation around the future options for post – as I set out briefly in my short final contribution.

...the art, science and 'magic' of communications and physical logistics... no longer need to rely on what happens at the post-office counter.

LOGISTICS VS FINANCIAL SERVICES: STRATEGIC CHOICE

Elmar Toime

E Toime Consulting Ltd

INTRODUCTION

How does the song go – 'What's love got to do with it'? Well, when we think about the post-office retail network today, what has the post got to do with it? Postal matters – the art, science and 'magic' of communications and physical logistics – no longer need to rely on what happens at the post-office counter. It is argued here that the strategies for postal businesses and for post-office businesses are diverging. These may already have reached the point of no return, with deep implications for postal policies.

BUSINESS MODELS FOR THE POST-OFFICE NETWORK

SEPARATION

In recent years, we have seen the growing organisational and ownership separation of the post-office retail network and postal logistics operations. Here, the term 'logistics' is used as a shorthand for mailing, parcel and associated services. The most recent example was the separation of Post Office Limited from the Royal Mail Group in the UK in order to allow Royal Mail's privatisation to go ahead. In practice, nothing much changed from a customer point of view. The two groups retain a mutual co-operation stance and a formal long-term contract. From a strategy point of view, Royal Mail may have some greater flexibility and it is no longer burdened with the social obligation of maintaining a widespread retail network. Maintenance of that network becomes a formal government policy position, subject either to direct or implicit subsidies or a post-office business plan that allows the group to pursue business strategies to ensure its financial sustainability.

This separation of the post-office network has existed for a number of years in the Netherlands and Germany. The retail network was transferred to the post bank operation. Stamp and parcel services are still provided under contract, but the primary purpose of these offices is to provide financial services.

STRATEGIC BUSINESS UNIT

In most countries where the postal company operates under a commercial mandate, the post-office retail network is usually managed as a separate business unit. In this model, it develops an independent set of services, typically in the financial services area, and acts as an agent for the mail and parcels operations. This has been a very successful approach because it recognises that the critical 'citizen need' being met is to support easy and economical access to banking and pension services, an aspect of central government policy. By operating as a profit centre, post-office management can focus on long-term sustainability. The aim is to remove dependence on subsidies and hidden cost allocations from the letter-mail monopolies. This has delivered real economic benefits to the parent postal company and to the community.

OPERATIONAL INTEGRATION

The founding purpose of the post-office network was to support postal operations. Mail services (stamps etc.) were purchased at the retail counter and delivery operations were integrated into the back office. This model still operates in some key markets, notably the United States, but is increasingly looking frail as a commercial solution.

In each of these models, the post office is expected to be a customer-facing agency, serving mainly small business and private clients. The postal services – stamps, parcels, registered and insured, and other value-added services – are sold on behalf of the logistics business units, whether mails or parcels and express. The post office has no say in pricing, service standards, complaints management or indeed business innovation. The value of these retail activities is a small part of total group revenue and is typically tightly regulated. So here we have a situation in which the customer-facing retail arm has no say in the mailing services provided for those customers.

DEVELOPMENT OF THE LOGISTICS BUSINESS

The language in the mails and parcels business of the modern postal company is now all about parcel logistics and e-commerce. Packets and large-format flats have become parcels. Today, there need to be many options for parcel delivery, from delivery to the door, to parcel shops (including post offices), to parcel lockers, to in-store collection. Selling of parcel services and parcel lodgement does require a physical presence. In this vigorously competitive area we find parcel terminals, parcel shops, online intermediaries and direct pick-up. Post offices still play a valuable role, especially for home trading businesses, but their cost structures are competing with many others. And the growth of parcel terminals inside post offices suggests the post office itself would prefer to direct its logistics customers away from the counter, where more valuable financial transactions may take place.

Thus, as postal companies increase their footprint in the logistics business, they are exposed to greater competitive forces. Prices and costs are under pressure and the ability to cross-subsidise or support an expensive post-office network becomes problematical. Transferring those problems to government by separating responsibility for the post-office network is logical.

DEVELOPMENT OF THE POST-OFFICE BUSINESS

In recent years, as letter-mail volumes have dropped, we have seen the financial results of quite a few postal companies become dependent on the financial services provided in post offices. Postal banks and postal insurance companies have been doing very well. Their conservative lending practices, implied government protection and conservative customers have allowed them to create strong, respected financial businesses. Combined with payment services and growing identification and central government business-process management, the post-office network has become resilient and less dependent on government protection and subsidy. The ability to manage the network in terms of a balance between company-owned and agency-operated franchises is a key element of future strategy. However, all these issues and strategic options for the post-office business have nothing to do with letters, parcels and logistics.

Whether a post-office company still owning and operating most of its outlets can survive without subsidy in the longer term is a separate question. But its existence is not about whether it can sell a few more parcel labels. It is about the sophistication, relevance and competitiveness of its financial and agency services. What's the post got to do with it?

SEPARATION OR UNION?

What are the strategic drivers of policy? There are strong arguments to justify a widespread post-office network to deliver a number of social services. It is mainly for these reasons that every country has some sort of obligation to maintain a network of a certain size and distribution. The logistics side of a postal business definitely benefits from this. It allows an effective interface for small business and citizens to buy postal services. The brand value of the post office itself is strong and contributes strength to the logistics business. In fact, 'post office' and 'postal company' are interchangeable brand names in the minds of the public. Where the principal business activity transacted in a post office relates to mailing services, then the mails and parcels operations have to carry that burden as a social obligation. But in any environment, the mail services being bought at the counter have features such as prices, delivery times and standards, and security-service add-ons which are controlled outside the post office.

Against this case for union are the business facts. A post-office network is expensive to run. It can hardly succeed on a marginal revenue, marginal cost basis. Its overheads and business systems have to be subsidised. In the few, exceptional instances where the business generated in post offices is dominant (for example, in the case of Poste Italiane), the logistics activity is small. Elsewhere, the debate within the post-office leadership group is about how to find growth, typically in financial and government services. That's fine, but what has the post got to do with it?

Where the retail network has been successful in recent years, postal managers have rightly pointed to the effectiveness of their business diversification strategies. Success of banking and insurance operations has cushioned the shock of letter-mail volume collapse. But increasingly, this seems to be a cross-subsidisation argument, not a business purpose argument. What is the postal company for? How can success in logistics and success in banking complement each other in the future? These are fundamental questions, for the boards of postal companies and for governments.

CONCLUSION

This has not been an argument against post offices. Where they have been able to carve out a role in financial services they have a solid strategic future. Whether that future is to be part of the 'old' postal company that delivers letters and parcels is the government policy question. In many cases, the need for the 'logistics' post to be less burdened by the 'post office' post has led to the diversification into financial services. Great, but once those services succeed and became dominant forces in their own right, what are the arguments to hold them together? The post should return to its origins – logistics. And the post-office network to its own separate future.

QUESTION FOR THOUGHT AND DISCUSSION

Is it possible to sustain a business argument that keeps the post-office network as an integral part of the postal logistics operation? If so, how can it be done?

Paradoxically, the more digital we become, the more we long for the physical.

NEW LIFESTYLES, NEW BUSINESS OPPORTUNITIES FOR POSTS

J.M. Melo

CTT Correios

INTRODUCTION

The world is going through a 'change of civilisation' paradigm shift which is affecting people's lifestyles in many ways. This is caused by very many factors and their joint effect is shaping a new society, with new needs.

WHY AND HOW LIFESTYLES ARE CHANGING

On the one hand, there are major trend factors like:

- The global financial/economic crisis and lower wages/income (which changes saving habits and rationalises money spending)

- The growing carbon footprint and ecological concerns (which modifies various consumers' routines)

- The scarcity of planetary resources, such as food, water and energy (which stresses the importance of 'how' and 'where' goods/things are manufactured)

- The growth in unemployment (which induces people to diversify their skills and competences in order to maximise their future job chances)

- The global population growth and tendency to live longer, and the resulting aging population (which raises different health/social welfare needs that require fulfilment).

These are resulting in greater instability, uncertainty, scarcity, stress, and a growing and aging population. They are troubling 'drivers' that require lifestyle adjustments.

On the other hand, ICTs (information and communication technologies) continue to undergo sophisticated and revolutionary developments which are having a faster and wider impact than ever before:

- The web is more and more accessible anywhere, anytime

- Increasingly smarter smartphones are outnumbering PCs and laptops

- Electronic information and/or data interchange is replacing physical communications for many purposes

- Electronic/dematerialised ways of payment (contactless or not) are popping out everyday

- 'The cloud' is enabling the greater democratisation of computing power, making it cheaper and more available everywhere and for everybody

- 3D printing is threatening to revolutionise the world of logistics and strengthen proximity and personalisation in the manufacturing process

- Social networks interconnect us (while providing extremely rich personal profiling insights)

- E-commerce promises to deliver (even via drones) anything to anyone, anyplace

- Self-driving vehicles are being tested in a number of world cities

- Geographic information systems (GIS) handle, interpret and visualise data in richer ways so as to enable the construction of useful relationships, patterns or trends which help to answer many questions

- Wearable technology[1] (such as wrist bands, glasses, smart tattoos, clothing, smart watches) provides tracking data on health, fitness, personal habits and routines

- Robots are taking charge in manufacturing sites (and even in our homes)

---

1   'Wearable technology, wearable devices, tech togs, or fashion electronics are clothing and accessories incorporating computer and advanced electronic technologies' (Wikipedia)

- Internet of Everything[2] (which encompasses the Internet of Things) is interconnecting anything and anyone

- Big data (because of IoT and IoE) is a kind of 'magic pot' spilling over with precious information (but whose transformation from raw material into useful knowledge has just begun. The power of analytics...).

The result of all this is that information and computer technologies (ICTs) are no longer 'guest stars in a supporting or enabling role', but are now stars on their own and they impact businesses and society in such a way that 'every business is a digital business'[3] and all people are affected.

So, how does all this affect people's lifestyles? There is:

- Great concern with *safety* (at various levels) and a need to minimise risk (this is particularly valid for retired people, urban professionals and Millennials[4]): now 'risk is the new evil and safety the new morality'[5]

- *Ubiquity* in space and time provided by web/social networks and materialised by the powerful smartphone (or other PDA), which makes people feel more and more empowered and wish to be interconnected continuously with each other

- Immersion into a world where (almost) everything is digital and can have a virtual representation, and this tends to create the demand for immediate satisfaction or gratification: the more *instantaneous*, the better

- The rhythm of modern life, which makes it difficult to harmonise work, family, friends and leisure activities; therefore producing a need for *convenience*

- A plethora of different goods and services that can be ordered and purchased via the web, which goes hand in hand with the need to be sure that whoever one is interfacing with *can, really, be trusted.*

Paradoxically, the more digital we become, the more we long for the physical. In fact, the more 'we buy apps, e-books, downloads, and as digital screens become our

---

2   IoE – Internet of Everything [interconnects people, processes, data and things (IoT – Internet of Things)]

3   Accenture Technology Vision 2014

4   People (Generation Y) born from 1980 onward, brought up using digital technology and mass media

5   www.slideshare.net/futurefoundation/global-trends-2014-future-foundation

default interface with the world, we seem to increasingly seek out physical objects and experiences... The ease with which we can access anything anytime and the *intangible format, tend to make digital things feel less valuable and special than their physical counterparts*[6].

HOW DO POSTS RESPOND TO THIS CHANGING WORLD?

So why should posts respond to all these major trends and changes to continue to meet people's new lifestyles expectations? And how should they do it?

Why do posts need to respond to this new world? Due to the 'substitution' effect any postal organisation will tend to reinvent itself (also) as a 'digital intermediary'[7]. Besides, through their networks made up of diversified and extensive physical, digital and human resources, posts normally have the capability – through a wise combination and integration of the digital and physical worlds – to materialise this intermediation for people (and organisations) in a convenient and trustful way.

How can they do this? The following are some examples of what posts can offer to match these new lifestyles (some of which are already in place, but most are likely to emerge, evolve and become more sophisticated):

A CENTRAL REPOSITORY OF DEMATERIALISED INFORMATION AND DATA

Trust is the most important intangible asset that posts possess and is immensely valued by everyone. Nowadays, all the data – the Big Data – that people are collecting via all the wearable technology, in many cases, is being channelled to as many different and separate 'repositories' (usually mobile apps) as the number of manufacturers that build these devices. The result of this is that, with different apps, each typically takes care of the data collected through each different device.

Why not enable platforms like the ones that many posts already have (e.g. E-Postbrief, viaCTT, Digipost etc.[8]) also to receive and safely record that data? More important than this, why not develop analytics that study all this data and discover unsuspected correlations and hidden patterns – thereby providing useful information for their owners? Besides, this information could also be used by posts

---

6   J. Walter Thompson Cpy reports (2013): 'The future of Correspondence' and 'Embracing Analog: why physical is hot'

7   'ICTs, Internet and postal operators' (Matthias Finger) [Reflections on the Postal Innovation Platform Conference 2013]

8   E-PostBrief (Deutsche Post), viaCTT (CTT/Portugal), Digipost (Norway Post)

for direct marketing purposes (based on previous consent and always granting people's anonymity, of course). This could turn out to be as useful for locating 'physical people' as GIS is in 'physical locations'.

E-COMMERCE ENHANCEMENTS

Regardless of the myriad of sites where one can buy (almost) anything, new lifestyles demand solutions that are able to, for instance: provide timely information about parcels' whereabouts, properly manage returns, offer quick and cheap delivery options, adjust themselves to different options in relation to different delivery locations, offer the widest range of delivery time options, and be trusted for payment security. Here are a few examples:

- Intelligent products/parcels – There are already solutions being tested or in place able to provide information about the integrity of parcels (even without needing to unwrap them[9]) or to monitor the freshness of goods until the moment they are delivered[10]. Others are developing solutions that will allow buyers to interact with their orders almost until they are delivered – this is all about enabling the order to instruct the delivery operator about the new drop-off point instead of the buyer[11].

- New types of logistics for new lifestyles, usually associated with 'smart people'[12], meaning customers who are more informed and more demanding. This means also new types of logistics are needed that address people's concerns and specific requirements which are, in turn, the consequence of increasing stress on the need for convenience and personalisation. Some examples include: Manufacturer-to-Consumer Logistics, Urban Logistics, Consumer Logistics, and Convenience Logistics[13].

---

9   DropTag® monitors impacts and vibrations, see www.cambridgeconsultants.com/droptag/ condition-monitoring

10 Infratab (Oxnard, California), 'an RFID technology startup, developed a SW solution based on smart sensors and RFID technology, to deliver better and more precise metrics about the condition of perishables'.

11 'Products that deliver themselves' (a James & James Fulfilment and the University of Cambridge project)

12 'Self-decisive, independent and aware citizens – smart people' (www.smart-cities.eu/model. html)

13 Logistics Trend Radar (a DHL Costumer Solutions & Innovation publication)

- Subscription models – Simplicity is the trend and therefore some e-retailers are offering subscription models[14] to their customers instead of charging for each purchase. For certain type of goods (examples are groceries and books) and services (recurrent buys), this is a way modern lifestyles find convenient (and perhaps most economic). It could prove to be worthwhile for posts to explore the benefits of extending this same model to the agreements (for delivery and logistic purposes) they contract with e-retailers and e-merchants.

- Multi-purpose parcel stations – The e-commerce boom is largely premised on the belief that convenience is critical. Parcel stations are PUDO (pick-up/drop-off) points that many posts have been wisely deploying in their territories. To strengthen the business case for these stations, it may be possible to explore other services (examples are documents and registered mail delivery, provision of financial services via 'embedded' ATM/Internet kiosks) and also consider how they could be 'rented' by owning posts to other operators. Parcel stations, if they are 'intelligent' and versatile enough, can be a kind of future post-office station.

- Unmanned deliveries – Drones seem to be the ultimate weapon either for urgent medical deliveries in congested urban centres[15], for speedy document deliveries[16] or for deliveries in areas poorly served by communications infrastructures (such as some parts of Africa)[17]. It's too soon to establish if there is a solid business case supporting their usage and if all the legal/regulatory requisites are fulfilled; however, many organisations (postal and non-postal) are conducting pilots or already running large-scale operations[18]. Self-driving vehicles are also being tested[19] which can revolutionise delivery operations: just imagine automatic vans or trucks specially designed for transporting goods (instead of people).

---

14 Similar to the ones cable TV operators already offer to customers: TV + Internet + Phone (triple pay).

15 In 2013, in Bonn, a test drone ('Paketkopter') flew a medicine package from a pharmacy to DHL headquarters.

16 The United Arab Emirates (UAE) plan to fly drones (2015) to deliver identity cards, driving licences and other permits.

17 matternet.us

18 For more information, refer to www.postalvision2020.com/2014/01/drone-makers/ and to 'Air Support' by Paul Willis in *Postal Technology International* (March 2014).

19 Such as Google, Mercedes-Benz, Lexus, BMW and Volvo

- Escrow role – Nowadays electronic means of payment (contactless or not) are widespread, both at brick-and-mortar retailers and when using any e-commerce site. In a dematerialised ecosystem like the web, payment security is critical and SW/HW sophisticated tools contribute to this; but as trusted third parties, even in this high-tech era, posts can act as escrow entities: they can receive the payments and only upon e-buyer's confirmation of proper goods' delivery, they will transfer the money to the e-retailer.

REVERSE HYBRID MAIL SOLUTIONS FOR CITIZENS

Many postal operators already offer electronic mailboxes via platforms[20] where one can receive – in digital format – mail from a number of previously selected senders (usually utilities and governmental agencies). For paper mail, posts can digitise the envelope and – bearing in mind the urge for convenience in modern lifestyles – can make the output available via mobile app; then it is up to the receiver's convenience to decide the next step:

- Envelope (plus contents) destroyed or recycled, or

- Full message (envelope plus contents) sent to postal address, and/or

- Digitalised copy of both envelope and contents sent to electronic mail box.

PROXIMITY SERVICES / WELFARE DISTRIBUTION

People are living longer but this also means that, in spite of modern health-care and medical attention, their mobility is likely to be diminished (in some cases severely), which means that they tend to stay at home. Partnerships between posts and governments can be established for providing, via mailmen, either proximity or welfare-distribution services in order to attend to the special needs of older people (not only supplying medication but also rendering other services)[21].

ENHANCED DIRECT MARKETING (DM)

Modern lifestyles appreciate personalisation. Very often, this is precisely what doesn't happen with digital DM messages and that's why most of us usually immediately delete them out of our email inbox, even without opening them. Conversely, paper-based DM messages – especially when carefully designed – tend to survive longer and also, perhaps, because of the sense of physical nostalgia they

---

20   E-PostBrief (Deutsche Post), viaCTT (CTT/Portugal), Digipost (Norway Post)

21   Examples: Denmark Post – Velfærdsdistribution (welfare distribution); La Poste (France) – FACTEO

convey and sensorial experience they induce. Besides, the inclusion of QR codes, augmented reality (AR) and video messages (displayed via super-slim LCD screens embedded into the physical DM object)[22] – that's to say, wisely combining the digital and the physical – can stress the modernity, attractiveness, relevance and personalisation of these objects. Then finally, who else to deliver them but the posts?

IDENTITY CONFIRMATION

Modern lifestyles are characterised by intensive digital/electronic interchanges and for most of these (for example, money transfers) it's vital to confirm the identity of those involved. For this, special digital certificates are used: for example, Qualified Digital Certificates. Due to legal dispositions, for issuing these certificates, a previous *in-person-proof* protocol has to be verified and, for this, physical confirmation of the DC owner's identity is mandatory. Again, this is something that posts are in a very good position to do (either at the counter of a post-office station or via postmen) and many are now offering services of this kind.

CONCLUSION

As society and ICT applications evolve, people's lifestyles also change and, as a result, new forms – and needs – of communication and interaction emerge. We have seen examples of possible solutions posts can explore and adopt or enhance to stay in business by designing an encompassing offer that fully matches those needs and constantly adapts itself vis-à-vis the sociological and technical trends that continue to shape our lives and our experience.

QUESTION FOR THOUGHT AND DISCUSSION

In view of the major societal and ICT trends outlined here, how can the postal industry react quickly and effectively to the future needs of its customers? Might it even anticipate these needs? What challenges does this pose for strategic planning and product/service development?

---

22 Future Transparent Electronics (e.g. www.corning.com) and Paper Electronics (e.g. http:// www.cenimat.fct.unl.pt/) developments will expand the possibilities.

What is true for the digital services of posts can be true for postal data coming from traditional activities.

DIGITAL STRATEGIES OF POSTS: WHAT'S NEXT?[1]

Olaf Klargaard and Philippe Régnard

Digital Division, *La Poste*

INTRODUCTION

Many posts have been developing relevant and promising digital solutions for consumers, like the digital mailbox, online payment solutions, authentication or secured archiving services. Various reasons led to this strategic move. A natural one is the fact that posts are historically positioned as leading providers of trusted communications services. For many posts, going digital is also a defensive move, after years of electronic substitution and decline in mail volumes.

This is a review of current directions and outlines some perspectives of potential developments in the digital field, especially given that, to date, digital initiatives have not been financially successful for most posts. Our view is that drops in mail volume should not lead postal operators to give up their know-how and assets in the physical world. The best digital strategies will help posts build bridges between Internet-based services and their network of mailboxes, outlets and postmen.

However, product innovation is only a first step when entering a new segment: the route (and time) to market is also key to success, especially in the digital age. Successful transformation of posts lies in the capacity to interact with partners and customers in a broader ecosystem. Rather than proposing their digital services exclusively through proprietary applications and websites, posts should build an

---

1   The views expressed in this chapter are those of the authors and should not be attributed to La Poste or ma-residence.fr.

openness strategy. This will allow posts to reinvent a business model based on their core activity while benefiting from the creativity of the crowd[2].

NATURAL STRATEGY FOR POSTS: BUILD DIGITAL SOLUTIONS ON THEIR TRUSTED BRAND

Engaging in the digital world as a trusted third party by providing credibility and security to web-based transactions and communications is a natural option for posts. If some posts were reluctant, fearing that digital solutions would cannibalise their core business, most operators have launched digital services in the early 2000s. In less than fifteen years, posts have shown their know-how as trusted third parties in the digital field by providing:

- Pure digital products as a natural transfer of traditional mail products (i.e. certified e-letters, registered e-letter, digital mailbox)
- Services securing online transactions and communications (i.e. secure identity verification, time stamping services, electronic signature).

The 'postal' brand as a trusted third party was the key asset supporting this strategy. Posts have protected the secrecy of correspondence in the physical communication world for centuries, securely delivering millions of legally binding mail (registered mail) handled by thousands of trusted postmen. Consequently, respect of confidentiality, data protection and privacy are properly and logically associated with postal brands.

This positioning is supported by the status of posts, as many are still state-owned enterprises. Government support to national postal operators, though it differs from one country to another, often constitutes an advantage for posts in the digital arena. An interesting example is Eboks, the secured digital mailbox solution launched by the Danish Post. Along with the development of the service, the Danish government has issued regulations requiring Danish businesses and citizens to communicate with the administration through Eboks. Undoubtedly, this kind of government support helps.

The economic and social weight of national postal operators is also generating confidence: significant revenues and investments, broad national presence and missions of public service (sometimes even fulfilled by civil servants).

---

2   [2] This model of development is well described by Collin & Verdier in *L'âge de la multitude – Entreprendre et gouverner après la révolution numérique* (2012) Armand Colin.

However, these assets could be more uncertain than might be expected. First, the postal brand may not be sufficient in itself to transform posts into recognised trusted third parties in the digital world. Trust is not necessarily transferable from one market segment to another: would you prefer your national postal operator or Gmail for managing your e-mails? Would you use an e-commerce platform recently developed by your postal company rather than ordering on Amazon? Secondly, it would be hazardous for posts to expect unconditional support from public authorities at a time where governments let competition play its role and select the best providers through tendering processes. Posts are well aware that legal monopoly protection is not open ended. Current regulatory constraint, notably on universal service provision, has even constituted an obstacle to postal innovation. Posts are incentivised to focus on universal service obligation based on universal delivery of D+1 physical mail, not necessarily in line with citizens' needs, and to maintain costly related infrastructure.

Considering these uncertainties, posts should rather focus on structural product advantages.

THE NEED TO ASSOCIATE DIGITAL POSTAL SERVICES WITH CORE PHYSICAL ASSETS

Though the development of digital solutions is a great opportunity for the postal sector, the risk with purely digital solutions like digital mailboxes, online payment solutions or authentication services is that similar offers can be – and are – proposed by competitors without any entry barriers connected to posts' physical assets. These services are replicable by purely digital players (see for instance Ecomail, Dropbox or Paypal for online payment solutions).

Posts can be more successful in solutions building bridges between physical processes (collection, delivery) and online services. In this way, posts may be able to gain a strong position on the market, while leveraging their core physical assets.

A good example is *YouPost*, the New Zealand Post digital mailbox service. Like most digital mailboxes, it enables customers to store documents, receive and archive mail, and to access the service from anywhere and any device. But it also offers consumers the capacity, in a single click, to send or receive documents by email *and* physical mail. With this feature, NZ Post provides the next-mile delivery solution and the service gets highly differentiated from the other digital mailboxes on the market.

Another example is connected delivery mailbox[3] experimentation, currently led by

---

3   See Ambrosini and Klargaard in *Reinventing the Post*, 2013

the French Post, that allows addressees to use their mailbox as usual (i.e. to receive mail and parcels) but also to benefit from additional services (reverse logistics, mailbox sharing) thanks to distance control of access rights through smartphones.

In the US, some economists[4] have illustrated the integration of core postal services and digital solutions by proposing authentication services that could be provided by extensive retail networks and in-person proofing experience. With thousands of post offices throughout the country, posts could provide more opportunities for in-person ID verification than any private-sector firm. This service could be used largely on the Internet to secure identity in transactions (notably on e-commerce and peer-to peer platforms).

'Disruptive innovation' in the postal sector will come from these innovative solutions. But more importantly, successful commercialisation and spread of usages will depend on the way it is developed, made available to developers and consumers, and part of a flourishing digital ecosystem.

AN OPEN MODEL: THE CONDITION FOR MARKET SUCCESS
INNOVATIVE PRODUCTS ARE NOT ENOUGH: INTEGRATION IN AN ECOSYSTEM IS KEY

Even if posts provide the best digital solutions, they may never reach consumers if they do not build capabilities to interact in a larger ecosystem. If the strategic choice is to sell and distribute these digital solutions exclusively through postal websites and applications, the plan seems doomed to failure. To be successful online, the product you are selling is as important as the way it is delivered to consumers and the way it is leveraged by partners.

The idea of a digital postal platform, developed by many postal economists and professionals[5], addresses this issue. This platform could be the place where the post provides key applications (address management, secured digital mailbox, authentication and online payment services, for example) that would be made available to consumers but also to developers, so that new functionalities and

---

4   See Laraine Balk Hope, Bruce Marsh and Virgil Ian Stanford, 'Peer-to-Peer Digital Commerce: Implications and Opportunities for the U.S. Postal Service and Other Posts', 2013

5   See Parker and Alstyn (2013) 'A digital Postal Platform: definitions and a roadmap'; Adra and Alii (2012) 'Universal service 2.0 on a digital postal Platform'; Asher and Alii (2011) 'The postal service role in the digital age – expanding the postal platform'; or Verdier and Colin (2012) *L'âge de la multitude – Entreprendre et gouverner après la révolution numérique*, Armand Colin, pp.153, 158

services would be built upon the basic layers of the platform. Posts would then develop and promote other applications from leading technology developers.

Open does not mean free. This model would create additional value as developers build applications for the installed base, for which posts would receive increased sales and downstream royalties from the increased transactions.

An open model also does not necessarily imply the need to build a platform. A simple way to open up to third-party developers is by having a public set of Application Programming Interfaces (APIs) which offer external developers the possibility to create new channels and services from postal data and solutions. APIs can be described as communication tools between two interfaces (software, applications and websites). An API is a set of rules and specifications that a software program can follow to access and make use of the services and resources provided by another particular software program that implements that API. An API can be developed for a restricted group of users (internal users in a company, defined partners) or it can be released to the public.

Public APIs are available to external developers who, in their websites, can integrate solutions and mobile applications data and services included in the API. For example, the USPS has made available on its website an API that allows developers to integrate in their websites the USPS service of printing shipping labels. The API makes this service widely available to users and relies on a community of external developers to innovate and associate new services.

OPEN MODELS ARE CRITICAL IN EXTENDING USAGE AND GENERATING REVENUES

Open models – whether an ambitious platform strategy or simply opening a wide set of public APIs – are a necessity in the digital age. First, they encourage third-party innovations and pull in ideas that posts would not otherwise have considered. For example, some external developers may integrate a secured document archiving service of a post with big-data-related solutions where the customer can provide data on demand to get commercial offers.

Second, they create new routes to markets for consumers, since developers will create new ways and places to access postal services and data. For example, a third party may develop an Android or IOS applications where posts have not.

Since APIs can contain information on how to use the service, restrictions and payment conditions (an API is a technical link between two interfaces but is also a contract), posts can rely on the creativity of the crowd to innovate on its services and data. Making public APIs available makes it possible to industrialise partnerships since developers connect to your services with no need of individual contracts of partnership.

Open models can then extend usage but also generate significant new revenue streams. In the USPS example below (print shipping label service), the API is obviously free to use, since the USPS has an obvious interest in thousands of websites (e-merchants, for example) integrating this functionality in their environment. But APIs can also integrate a fee each time the service (or the data) is used via the API. This would be the case, for example, for an API proposing an address verification service, where posts could generate revenue each time the service is used from any connected website or application.

CONCLUSION

Diversification of postal activities toward digital products and services is key for postal operators to survive in the long term. These new services should be built on postal physical assets to bring value to consumers and to differentiate them from 'pure digital'. The key condition for success, however, is the way these services will be made available to partners and customers: an open model of innovation is definitely a must have.

Beyond digital services, open models constitute an opportunity for posts to create new business models. What is true for the digital services of posts can be true for postal data coming from traditional activities. Posts are currently using open APIs on a very limited set of data. With millions of operations in post offices, the transport information of mail, parcels and trucks, and data that can be collected by thousands of postmen, posts clearly have an opportunity and interest to create a structure that makes these datasets available to external developers for integration in their own websites, applications and solutions. This could well constitute a major revenue stream in tomorrow's postal models.

QUESTION FOR THOUGHT AND DISCUSSION

The authors maintain that 'Diversification of postal activities toward digital products and services is key for postal operators to survive in the long term'. If this is the case, where is the profitable business to be found and what are the risks associated with these kind of diversification?

The postal industry faces tremendous challenges and posts must be aware that new market needs and customer demands may outrun their innovative capabilities in research and development.

AN OPEN PLATFORM FOR THE POSTAL SECTOR

Bernhard Bukovc

Postal Innovation Platform

INTRODUCTION

In recent years the search for innovation, new business models and additional revenue streams in the postal industry has increased considerably. The drivers behind these developments are obvious: mail volume decline, ICT developments leading to mail substitution, changing consumer behaviour and new market demands. Posts are facing a multitude of challenges and the search for new revenue streams bears many risks, but equally opportunities.

Traditionally postal operators have cooperated very closely. This is rooted in their common history as state entities that are not in competition with each other. This situation has now changed in many regions and countries. Posts have found themselves in the new role of market players competing with each other and new entrants, mainly in those regions where markets have been liberalised. However, despite this, posts still need to cooperate closely in order to provide their services, which do not stop at the country border.

Today, we see various structures, organisations and forms of cooperation and the question is whether these are adequate in order to respond successfully to today's challenges. Or is there a need for an additional, new way of cooperating and, if so, what could this new approach look like?

COOPERATIVE APPROACHES

Postal operators tend to follow different approaches depending on the required solutions. On the cooperative side we can identify three approaches: unilateral, bilateral and the multilateral approach.

UNILATERAL APPROACH

Every post, like any other business entity, works on its own strategy and business plans in order to reach its business objectives. The unilateral approach focuses on the particular needs and strategies through which the respective post develops new services, innovative solutions or enters into new business areas. Posts will look at what other posts are doing and they will probably exchange with other stakeholders before implementing something new, but the focus in most cases is on the geographical business area in which that particular post operates. It will probably work together or consult with the government and other domestic customers or stakeholders. This may apply for technical solutions, new products or entire new business areas. In essence, the postal operator will develop a service or solution that fits with its particular needs in the domestic market or its international strategy.

BILATERAL APPROACH

In some cases, posts have an interest in extending their focus to another market, which may be due to an already-existing strong business relationship with the other country. In these cases, posts will follow a bilateral approach and will try to develop a solution together with another post. One business area in which we can see such cooperative approaches today, for example, is e-commerce. Several posts have developed solutions with other posts, often in neighbouring countries, in order to implement cross-border e-commerce services. The main drivers behind such cooperative solutions are business opportunities and the need to create a seamless cross-border service for customers, an element that is still missing in most cross-border e-commerce offerings. The advantage of such a bilateral approach is the possibility of working on and implementing a solution or service relatively quickly because only the technical requirements and operations of two posts are involved. This allows not only a speedier process, but also the alignment of only two operations, which is less complicated than a similar approach on a multilateral level. The disadvantage is that only two posts are involved and that the solution might not work with regard to other countries or regions.

MULTILATERAL APPROACH

Multilateral approaches are necessary for several services and solutions in order to allow the exchange of mail or parcels in the cross-border business. Posts need to cooperate on a basic level in order to create the global postal network. Technical standards, payment mechanisms and calculation models for the items handed over to another post are just a few examples of areas where posts must work together. In reality, this cooperation goes much further. The Universal Postal Union (UPU) not only guarantees that these minimal requirements are met, but through continuous work via the respective UPU bodies and working groups, postal operators around the world try to identify market needs and develop appropriate and respective solutions. The e-commerce challenge is currently one of the key topics with which postal operators have to deal because one of the new market requirements, namely, a seamless cross-border solution and consumer experience, is still not widely implemented. Also, other associations and organisations such as the International Post Corporation (IPC) or the Kahala group, together with smaller groups of postal operators, develop solutions that support the interoperability of different posts. Most of these organisations have in common that they develop solutions with and for their respective members, which are postal operators. The UPU has a wider focus because it also involves governments.

However, in such processes, important market players such as consumer organisations, suppliers, academics and others are often only consulted at certain stages in the process, but usually not directly involved from the beginning. Postal operators tend to commission studies through which they try to understand better the market needs, and they work with one or more suppliers when it comes to implementing a new solution; but the relationship and cooperation between all these different stakeholders could go much deeper, thus enabling and facilitating completely new solution-finding processes.

DEFICIENCIES AND ADVANTAGES OF THE DIFFERENT APPROACHES

With increasing competition, the opportunities to cooperate are limited. However, every industry faces the same dilemma and despite fierce competition most industry sectors have found ways to cooperate and develop products and solutions together. This saves costs, making better use of scarce resources, and the combination of different strengths and knowledge often creates better products and services.

Looking at the postal industry, there are some advantages of developing solutions and services independently (i.e. without the involvement of others). One of the drivers is a possible competitive advantage. Another one would be a straight-forward process that allows the post to focus solely on its own requirements and develop a service tailored to its specific needs.

However, there are also some considerable deficiencies in such an approach. First, as mentioned above, other stakeholders might not be involved adequately. This may be the case when other posts are not involved and a cross-border element is not adequately considered. It may be difficult and costly to integrate such an element at a later stage, or change the operational processes. Second, posts may run the risk of duplicating mistakes that others have made or identified already. Third, some elements may not be addressed adequately and reflected in the final product or service because some stakeholders, whether domestic or international, have not been involved. And fourth, the postal operator may miss business opportunities because it does not identify business potentials or it has insufficiently studied the best ways and processes in the implementation process itself.

THE 'OPEN PLATFORM'

In order to avoid the deficiencies mentioned above, an 'open platform' approach could be a way to minimise risks and exploit more business opportunities. Such an approach would not replace existing processes, but it could help better to integrate and link these processes together, thus facilitating the development and implementation of new products, services and solutions.

ABOUT OPEN PLATFORMS

The idea of open platforms is rooted in the concept of open innovation, a term created by Professor Chesbrough that describes a strategic innovation approach which includes partners, thus sharing risks and benefits.[1] This concept is based upon the contention that companies should use external ideas as well as internally sourced ideas, and external as well as internal paths, as the company tries to

---

1   For more details on open platforms and open innovation please see Henry William Chesbrough's *Open Innovation: The new imperative for creating and profiting from technology* (Boston: Harvard Business School Press, 2003) and 'The era of open innovation' (*MIT Sloan Management Review*, 2003); Andrea Zeller's 'Is open innovation a sustainable option for the postal sector?' (*EPFL, the Network Industries Quarterly*, Vol. 13, No. 2, 2011); and the websites http://www.innovationinthecrowd.com and http://postal-innovation.epfl.ch (the website of the Postal Innovation Platform).

advance its technology and develop new solutions. In essence, the concept questions the capabilities of business entities that rely only on their own research and development, and thus may be unable to identify full market potential and acquire necessary knowledge. The concept of an open platform is a managerial process including sources of different kind, such as other companies, customers, academic institutions, governments or other stakeholders. It uses these external as well as internal sources to identify opportunities and develop innovative services, products and solutions. A further element that is relevant in this context is the two-way approach, which essentially means that open innovation allows innovation and new ideas to move into the company and its development processes and also for ideas to move outward (i.e. to be used by other market players).

AN OPEN PLATFORM FOR THE POSTAL SECTOR

Open platforms that exploit the opportunities presented by open innovation strategies obviously can change the way of researching and developing innovative products, services and solutions in the postal sector. As described above, postal operators often have followed different and more limited approaches in their strategies, involving to a larger or smaller degree other market players and stakeholders. However, the deficiencies and risks of more limited approaches may hinder postal operators from optimally identifying and exploiting business opportunities. Individual activities limited to in-house resources risk overlooking important developments and will often either copy what is happening somewhere else or simply repeat and duplicate processes and even sometimes repeat the mistakes of other companies.

The Ecole Polytechnique Fédérale de Lausanne (EPFL), the Universal Postal Union (UPU) and Swiss Post have identified the need to establish new ways of innovating and exploiting market opportunities through using an open innovation platform. In 2013, the three partners launched the Postal Innovation Platform (PIP), an open platform that invites all postal industry stakeholders, including postal operators, governments, customers, suppliers, industry associations and others, to join forces and research and develop innovative services, products and solutions.

Adopting the principles of open innovation, the platform allows partners to identify topics, bring in knowledge, research and ideas, and to combine and work on these items in order to develop solutions and innovative services and products. The output should benefit all participating entities, either through implementing the findings and results in their own organisations or through the development of international solutions.

The development of common solutions and exchange of findings is one of the key advantages of the postal innovation platform and will not only provide the opportunity to join forces and save costs, but also to develop solutions that one operator would not have been able to develop independently. In order to formalise the processes and allow relevant and interested parties to come together, the platform organises regular meetings, the so-called 'PIP Roundtables', which focus on topics that the involved stakeholders agree upon. Industry stakeholders can identify the topics they are interested in and join the respective roundtables and working groups. They can share their experiences and knowledge and can gain from the experience and knowledge shared by others; in addition, they can work together on innovative ideas and solutions, thus creating additional value.

CONCLUSION

The postal industry faces tremendous challenges and posts must be aware that new market needs and customer demands may outrun their innovative capabilities in research and development. To avoid this danger, more cooperation is an essential element in the search for innovative ideas, products, services and business or operative solutions. Open innovation models have shown that there are clear advantages for all parties involved. An open innovation platform allows postal operators to optimise external and internal sources, exchange with relevant stakeholders and so identify possibilities and potentials that postal operators would not be able to identify alone. In addition, an open innovation platform helps to speed up processes, which is essential in an environment of significant market developments and fast-moving consumer behaviour changes. In this way, the Postal Innovation Platform can become a valuable tool and asset of the postal industry, to increase the level of innovation and to develop products, services and solutions the market demands.

QUESTION FOR THOUGHT AND DISCUSSION

What are the barriers to wider co-operation between posts in such an open innovation platform? What other benefits may be gained from expanding the platform to include players from other sectors?

CONTINUALLY REINVENTING THE POST

Derek Osborn
Whatnext4u

As its title suggests, this second edition of *Reinventing the Post* has focused on 'changing postal thinking'. Of course, this phrase can be interpreted in different ways. If read in a passive way, it may be understood as an observation that 'thinking' in the postal world is changing – and the contributions in this book have certainly illustrated the many ways in which that is happening. If 'changing postal thinking' is considered in a more active way, then this book could be seen as playing a role in helping to change thinking in the postal world. I am sure that it will do some of that as well. Both functions are important and will make the many efforts that have gone into this book worthwhile.

These issues are clearly of vital importance for everyone who works in the wider postal sector, for their jobs and their future, and need to be discussed, openly and robustly. For leaders and managers in the industry, the ideas in this book can help to provide the background and thinking for important decisions about strategy and direction. For students or training programmes across the sector, this book can be used as a text to stimulate discussion and learning. The questions at the end of each contribution are designed particularly for that purpose.

Whatever your reason for reading about the future of the postal industry and how it is now being reinvented in so many different ways around the globe, you can be certain of one thing: there are enough enthusiastic, energetic and innovative people in the wider industry, with diverse talents, entrepreneurial skills and enormous drive and determination, to ensure that the business of reinventing the post will not only continue but probably expand and accelerate.

The one outstanding theme that will have to emerge more strongly and is a foundation for everything else will be that of *sustainability*. It is one thing for the posts to have survived the seismic changes happening all around, and within, them; but it is quite another to *build a sustainable business* and to ensure that it will be there for generations to come, as part of a sustainable world. Maybe that it is a topic for another edition!

CONTRIBUTORS

Dr Wolfgang Baier has been advising and driving SingPost's transformation for 10 years, first in his previous capacity as a McKinsey partner and, since 2011, as GCEO. He comes from the third generation of a family with a postal history, following his grandfather and mother into the industry. Under Wolfgang's leadership, the SingPost Group accelerated its transformation, focusing on three key thrusts: business model transformation, innovation & technology, and people engagement & culture.

Dr Christoph Beumer is Managing Partner and Chairman of the Board of Directors of the BEUMER Group in Beckum. He holds a degree in mechanical engineering with a focus on conveyor technology from the University of Hanover. He has worked at BEUMER since 1992 and has headed this family-owned company since 2000.

Bernhard Bukovc has worked for the postal and logistics industry for over 15 years, including his employments at Austria Post and the International Post Corporation. He is now an independent consultant and the Chairman of the Postal Innovation Platform, an initiative of EPFL, UPU and other postal-industry stakeholders. He is also the founder and CEO of a European e-commerce platform for wine.

Shailendra Kumar Dwivedi is an officer of the Indian Postal Service and currently leading postal services in an upcoming region in India. He recently completed a four-year term as a faculty member at the Asian-Pacific Postal College, Bangkok where he designed and conducted courses on postal business management, innovation and leadership, among others. Now he is taking a break from training and putting his ideas into practice in India Post. E-mail: shailendra.dwivedi@gmail.com

Jean Philippe Ducasse is a French–American postal research, strategy and regulatory consultant active in North America and developing countries. He is currently a consultant to the United States Postal Service (USPS) Office of the

Inspector General. JP has previous experience with Pitney Bowes, the UPU (head of the QSF) and the EC. He also led Groupe La Poste's market research and international strategy teams. E-mail: jpducasse@uspsoig.gov

Michael Faltum has been Head of Production Technology at PostNord Danmark since 1997. He was educated as an engineer and has an MBA in technology management and a bachelor's in marketing. His main competences are: specialised IT (production IT), technology development, program management and lean production.

Steve Hannon is Chief Executive of PLCWW with over 40 years of experience in the postal industry. He is a former operations director of Royal Mail. Since leaving Royal Mail, Steve has worked for users, suppliers, operators and regulators in the postal industry, including Postcomm, Ofcom, Comreg, the EU, the CCK (Kenya) and India Post. He has also worked as interim chief executive and currently non-executive director of Guernsey Post.

Laraine Balk Hope is an economist at the United States Postal Service (USPS) Office of the Inspector General's Risk Analysis Research Center. She previously held executive positions at the USPS and in the private sector. While at USPS, she served as an expert witness in several dockets before the Postal Regulatory (formerly Rate) Commission. Laraine received an MBA from Yale and a BA from Wesleyan University. E-mail: lbhope@uspsoig.gov

As COO of SingPost, **Dr Sascha Hower** is responsible for strengthening all critical processes and implementing innovative elements of SingPost's accelerated transformation. In addition to his responsibility for Operations across the SingPost Group, Sascha oversees key customer-facing channels like the Post Office operations and Customer Service. Prior to SingPost, Sascha was a junior partner with McKinsey, focusing on operational transformations and performance turnarounds of several postal operators in Europe and Asia.

Juan Ianni has 40 years' experience in the postal industry, completing projects in 65 countries. After a career with USPS and the World Bank, he became a private consultant in 2004, focusing on postal-sector policy and regulatory issues. He has authored a number of postal-sector studies including the *Handbook of Postal Service Reform* (edited by Crew, Kleindorfer and Campbell) and *ICTs, New Services, and Transformation of the Post* (ITU/UPU, 2010).

Jacob Johnsen has made postal electronic services his focus, based on more than 25 years in the postal and telecommunications industries. Following years as a senior executive at the head of various companies, he decided to focus on strategic positioning of messaging and hybrid mail. A sought-after speaker and moderator, he is involved in many projects around the world within his areas of expertise. He holds several trusted positions in international networks including Chairman of the European Standardisation for Postal Electronic Services. E-mail: johnsen@ ipostes.com

Amine Khechfé is responsible for directing all aspects of the Endicia business unit as well as managing its position within the Newell Rubbermaid brands. Amine co-founded Endicia in 1987 and holds a BS in engineering from Worcester Polytechnic Institute and an MS in Engineering from Stanford University.

Adrian King has worked as a consultant to the postal and logistics industry for the last twenty-five years. During that time, he has had the privilege to work for 15 posts, numerous suppliers, international bodies, government and regulators.

Olaf Klargaard leads the digital mailbox solution of La Poste, Digiposte. Previously, he has developed partnerships with P2P and collaborative consumption platforms for ma-residence.fr, a social network gathering communities of neighborhoods. Before that, he led strategy and regulatory affairs at Pitney Bowes for Europe and worked as an economist for La Poste. Olaf holds a master's degree from Paris Dauphine University, ESSEC Business School and Paris Institute of Political Science.

Hans Kok is an independent postal consultant with 20 years' experience within Dutch Post and 20 years in his own global practice in restructuring of the postal sector since 1995. Hans has worked worldwide and in approximately 20 countries in Africa, for policy makers, operators and postal regulatory institutions. He was recently responsible for the study on the future of universal services in Africa for the African Union. E-mail: hankok@gmail.com

Janras Serame Kotsi is Group Executive at the SA Post Office with vast experience in the postal industry spanning over 30 years. He has been at the centre of the transformation of the mail business and successfully managed its ISO 9001:2008 accreditation. He is currently the chairperson of the SADC Postal Operations Directors' Forum and was instrumental in the launching of the successful regional SAPOA Postal Forum in 2013.

Graeme Lee is a senior partner in Sunflower Associates, which aims to place 'posts at the centre of development'. A leading postal development professional, with experience of working in more than 70 countries, he provides postal-sector policy, strategy, business planning and operational advice to governments and posts.

Erwin Lenhardt is Vice President Logistics & Postal Solutions with T-Systems, a globally leading IT Services provider. For more than 20 years, he held senior management positions with Siemens. In his management roles he has followed the post and parcel industry through contact with many senior decision makers, gaining a deep understanding of the industry's needs, strategies and vision. Lenhardt holds a German electrical-engineering degree and US MBA.

Gareth Locksley is a senior partner with Sunflower Associates. From 1999 to 2010, he was a member of the Global ICT Division of the World Bank, having joined from Cable & Wireless where he held various positions including Chief Economist with Mercury Communications. Gareth has also been an official of the Competition Directorate of the European Commission following an academic career. He has published widely on ICT and media issues.

As VP Customer Care & Excellence of SingPost, **Lily Loo** manages contact centres in Singapore, Manila and India across the organisation and its regional subsidiaries. In addition, she drives service quality on a global level within UPU's EMS unit. A Net Promoter Certified Associate, Lily is a strong customer-experience advocate. Prior to SingPost, Lily spearheaded the first outsourced offshore contact centre project for SingTel, Singapore's largest telecommunications company.

João Melo is Head of Innovation Management and Development within CTT (Correios de Portugal) Strategy & Development Directorate. He holds a degree in electrotechnical engineering from IST Lisbon. Previously he was Lecturer at Universidade Nova de Lisboa's Physics Department, Communications Network Manager at Direcção General de Correios, in CTT Portugal, and Project Manager at Marconi S.A.

Liene Norberg is a management consultant who works with strategic development and international expansion of SMEs in various industries. Currently working with the trading of biofuels, her focus is on extended leadership in the domain of sustainability. Partnering with Derek Osborn under umbrella of SCALE Advantage EEIG, a platform for cross-industry collaboration has been created, helping to scale-up social, environmental and economic sustainability within the postal sector.

Carla Pace is a senior postal analyst with Cullen International, with 13 years' experience in the postal sector. She has strong expertise in regulated industries, including working for the Belgian and Italian postal incumbents and other prominent institutions in Italy and Luxembourg. Carla has a PhD in economics, specialising in industrial organisation and regulation.

Maurizio Puppo is Sales Manager at Solystic. During his career he has worked at ENI (an Italian gas and oil company) and Elsag (a security and automation company). He held various roles in software development, product engineering, marketing and operations management. He has also published several books of fiction and literary criticism. E-mail: maurizio.puppo@solystic.com

Philippe Régnard graduated with a master's degree in political sciences at La Sorbonne University (Paris I) and began working as a public affairs and lobbying consultant (Boury – Tallon & Associés). He joined La Poste Headquarters as a regulatory expert, then in charge of the relations with competition and regulatory authorities and public administration. He is currently working at the Digital Division of La Poste Group as Director of Institutional relations.

Alain Roset is a realistic innovative manager who focuses on strategy of postal operators and technologies applied to logistics. His analyses are based on an involvement in the economics modelling for the delivery of mail, parcels, use of big data and some new electronic technologies applied to the mail and parcel market. He promotes the value of letters in coherence with new digital trends by developing open innovation methodology. E-mail: alain.roset@polytechnique.org

Priv.-Doz. Dr.-Ing. Eva Savelsberg is a member of the Executive Board of INFORM. Being Vice President Logistics Division, she is responsible for software systems which optimise elaborate logistics processes in real time via intelligent planning and dispatch decisions. The Logistics Division focusses on maritime and inland ports, distribution centres, building materials and retail. Eva is lecturer at the RWTH Aachen University where she received her PhD in Mechanical Engineering (2002). E-mail: eva.savelsberg@inform-software.com

Jeff Sibio is the Director, Industry Marketing for Transportation and Logistics at Intermec by Honeywell. He is considered to be a thought leader and known for his innovative, customer-first approach in transportation and logistics. Jeff assists companies globally in understanding best practice while also acting as a visionary, helping these companies imagine their own futures.

Ute Simon is Senior Consultant in the Logistics Division of INFORM. She has been working for INFORM since 1997, holding various positions within the company. As team leader and senior consultant, Ute is responsible for INFORM's yard automation systems in the field of parcel and distribution centres and acts as key account manager for all postal clients. In 2014, Ute completed her MBA at the University of Wales, Cardiff. E-mail: ute.simon@inform-software.com

Ian Streule is a partner at Analysys Mason Limited. He has over 16 years of experience in communications, media and technology consulting, including on postal-sector issues for regulators in the UK, Ireland and Kenya. Ian is an expert in communications regulation, economic costing and strategic advice, and he has served clients in most of Europe and in Africa, Asia, the Caribbean, South America and Oceania. E-mail: ian.streule@analysysmason.com

Kristina Survilė is Head of the Internal Control and Audit Department at Lithuania Post. She is also Quality Management Representative responsible for quality management at Lithuania Post. She has a master's degree in Business Administration (Kaunas University of Technology) and, since 2004, she has had a professional designation of certified internal auditor (CIA), granted by the Institute of Internal Auditors (IIA).

Elmar Toime was Chief Executive of New Zealand Post and Executive Deputy Chairman of Royal Mail. Now living in London, he has a life-time achievement award for leadership in the postal industry. He is founding chairman of Postea Inc. and is a member of the Deutsche Post DHL supervisory board.

Dr Herbert-Michael Zapf is President and CEO of International Post Corporation. IPC is owned by 24 member posts in Asia Pacific, North America and Europe, and provides services to more than 170 postal companies. He is also Professor of Strategic Management and International Business at Middlesex University in Brussels (UBI). He graduated from the University of Paris IX Dauphine and obtained his PhD from the University of Kassel.